Hildegard of Bingen

CISTERCIAN STUDIES SERIES: NUMBER TWO HUNDRED FIFTY-THREE

Hildegard of Bingen

Solutions to Thirty-Eight Questions

Translated by

Beverly Mayne Kienzle
with Jenny C. Bledsoe and Stephen H. Behnke

Introduction and Notes by

Beverly Mayne Kienzle
with Jenny C. Bledsoe

α

Cistercian Publications
www.cistercianpublications.org

LITURGICAL PRESS
Collegeville, Minnesota
www.litpress.org

A Cistercian Publications title published by Liturgical Press

Cistercian Publications

Editorial Offices
161 Grosvenor Street
Athens, Ohio 45701
www.cistercianpublications.org

A translation of the text in J.-P. Migne's *Solutiones*, Patrologia Latina 197:1037–54.

All Scripture quotations have been translated by Beverly Mayne Kienzle.

1   2   3   4   5   6   7   8   9

Library of Congress Cataloging-in-Publication Data

Hildegard, Saint, 1098–1179.
    [Solutiones. English]
    Hildegard of Bingen : solutions to thirty-eight questions / translated by Beverly Mayne Kienzle with Jenny C. Bledsoe and Stephen H. Behnke ; introduction and notes by Beverly Mayne Kienzle with Jenny C. Bledsoe.
        pages   cm. — (Cistercian studies series ; no. 253)
    "A translation of the text in J.-P. Migne's Solutiones, Patrologia Latina 197:1037-54."
    Includes bibliographical references and index.
    ISBN 978-0-87907-253-7 — ISBN 978-0-87907-753-2 (ebook)
    1. Bible—Criticism, interpretation, etc.—History—Middle Ages, 600–1500.   I. Kienzle, Beverly Mayne.   II. Title.   III. Title: Solutions to thirty-eight questions.
    BS511.3.H55   2014
    220.6—dc23   2014000247

Canis . . . aliquod commune et naturale sibi in moribus hominis habet, et ideo hominem sentit et intelligit, et eum amat, et libenter cum eo moratur, et fidus est.
Hildegard of Bingen, *Physica*

Ad Miam,
canem affectuosam et laetabundam

Ad memoriam
Snickers, Callie, et Honey
canum constantissimarum, charitativarum, et clementium

Contents

Abbreviations

CCCM   Corpus Christianorum, Continuatio
            Mediaeualis
CCSL   Corpus Christianorum, Series Latina
Guibert, *Epistolae*   Guibert of Gembloux. *Epistolae quae in*
            codice B.R. Brux. 5527–5534
            inueniuntur, 1
PL   Patrologiae cursus completus, series
            latina
SCh   Sources chrétiennes
Vulg.   *Biblia Sacra: iuxta Vulgatam uersionem*

Hildegard of Bingen's Works Cited

Cause   *Cause et cure*
Diu. operum   *Hildegardis Bingensis Liber diuinorum*
            operum
Epistolarium 1   *Hildegardis Bingensis Epistolarium.*
            Pars prima: I–XC
Epistolarium 2   *Hildegardis Bingensis Epistolarium.*
            Pars secunda: XCI–CCLR
Epistolarium 3   *Hildegardis Bingensis Epistolarium.*
            Pars tertia: CCLI–CCXC
Expl. Symb.   *Explanatio Symboli Sancti Athanasii*
Expo. Euang.   *Expositiones euangeliorum*
Homilies on
   the Gospels   *Homilies on the Gospels*
Letters 1   *Letters*. Vol. 1
Letters 2   *Letters*. Vol. 2

Letters 3	*Letters*. Vol. 3
Life of Hildegard	*The Life of the Saintly Hildegard by Gottfried of Disibodenberg and Theodoric of Echternach*
Opera minora	*Hildegardis Bingensis Opera minora*
Sciuias	*Hildegardis Sciuias*
Scivias (Eng.)	*Scivias*
Solutiones	*Solutiones triginta octo quaestionum*
Symph.	*Symphonia armonie celestium reuelationum*
Two Hagiographies	*Two Hagiographies: Vita Sancti Rupperti Confessoris and Vita Sancti Dysibodi Episcopi*
V. Hild.	*Vita Sanctae Hildegardis*
Vite mer.	*Hildegardis Liber Vite Meritorum*

Preface

HILDEGARD OF BINGEN'S writing of the *Solutions to Thirty-Eight Questions* took root in her friendship with Guibert of Gembloux, who was an ardent and unrelenting correspondent. He served as the secretary for the great visionary in the two years preceding her death. Guibert pressed Hildegard for solutions to questions on Scripture. She delayed, explaining that illness and the duties of governance left her with no time for writing the remaining solutions. The persistent questioner persevered, even writing to the whole community at Rupertsberg to beseech them to intercede for him. If Guibert had not pleaded with the seer relentlessly and then come to her aid, she probably would not have written or completed the *Solutions*.[1]

Hildegard's other works are not so closely tied to one person's goading and encouragement. Nonetheless, for her three major visionary works, she acknowledges the help she received from assistants. Hildegard's mentor and then-secretary Volmar intervened with the abbot of Disibodenberg to procure permission for her to write. Volmar and "a noble girl" (undoubtedly Richardis) assisted with the writing of *Sciuias*. Volmar and "a certain girl" helped the seer with the *Book of Life's Merits* and the beginning of the *Book of Divine Works*. Completing the *Book of Divine Works* seemed an overwhelming task after her secretary Volmar's death in 1173. The seer's nephew Wezelinus came to her aid himself, procured assistance from other "learned men," and then appointed Gottfried of Echternach as provost

---

[1] See the introduction below, 8–11, 15, on this correspondence.

of Rupertsberg. The epilogue to the *Book of Divine Works* attests that Ludwig, abbot of Saints Eucharius and Matthias in Trier, assisted Hildegard himself with corrections and, like Wezelinus, secured assistance for her through other "learned men."[2]

The translation of the *Solutions* likewise would not have seen print without the assistance of my students, and particularly Jenny Bledsoe. I assigned translations from the *Solutiones* during my fall 2011 course "Hildegard and the Gospels." The *Homilies on the Gospels* were published during that term; once they appeared, we moved from translating homilies to translating the *Solutiones* and reading additional homilies in English. I invited the students to join me in preparing a translation of this important and little-studied work. Christopher Evans generously sent the preprint version of his edition for us to read alongside the version in the *Patrologia Latina*. Two students responded with draft translations of as many *Solutions* as possible, which I used to compare with my own handwritten notes. While I am the principal translator of the text, the efforts of Jenny Bledsoe and Stephen Behnke made it possible to produce the whole. Jenny then helped me over the summer of 2012 to edit the translation, supply notes, and comment on the draft of the introduction. Other students took extra care in commenting on the texts, identifying Scripture, and exploring the background for the exegetical problems involved. Timothy Baker and Zachary Guiliano enriched our learning with their deep knowledge of the Scriptures. Katherine Wrisley Shelby expanded our theological discussions; Marina Connelly and Jaime Bonney performed and added to our knowledge of Hildegard's exegesis in song. Sasha Prevost and Robin Lutjohann enhanced our understanding of Hildegard's mystical ex-

---

[2] Beverly Mayne Kienzle, *Hildegard of Bingen's Gospel Homilies: Speaking New Mysteries*, Medieval Women: Texts and Contexts 12 (Turnhout: Brepols, 2009), 72–76 (hereafter, Kienzle, *Hildegard's Gospel Homilies*).

perience and the visual exegesis of her illuminations. Zachary Matus, teaching fellow, contributed to all of our discussions.

Jenny thanks Kel for listening to her vent about the some-times aggravating experience of translating Hildegard's Latin, her kitties Danny and Zooey for always supplying a welcome distraction, and her parents for their unending encouragement. As Hildegard demanded of her in a dream, Jenny hopes that this translation does justice to the original work of the newly canonized saint and Doctor of the Church. Jenny, along with all of Beverly's students, are ever grateful for the mentorship of their *magistra* and her eagerness to involve young scholars in her research projects.

My gratitude goes to Christopher Jarvinen, Maecenas of my research, whose generosity contributed to the uninterrupted work on the project during the summer of 2012. Father Mark Scott encouraged the project from the moment I first proposed it. Marsha Dutton graciously and expertly edited the completed text. Anita Dana offered one of her remarkable inspired paintings for the cover design. Linn Maxwell Keller's enthusiasm for Hildegard, the inspiration of her voice and witness, and the summer production of her DVD on the saint stimulated my energy. Last but never least, I thank my family members for the unfailing support they give: Edward and Kathleen, the felines Walter, Basile *dulcis memoriae*, Athena, Tecla, Cecilia, Stella—and Mia, newest and only canine member of the family.

Paraphrasing Hildegard's words, I pray that "all who helped me and consoled me as I toiled may rejoice."

Beverly Mayne Kienzle
Cambridge, Massachusetts
2014

Introduction

THE *SOLUTIONS TO THIRTY-EIGHT QUESTIONS*, perhaps the least studied of Hildegard of Bingen's writings, is translated here from the original Latin into English for the first time. In this work of exegesis, Hildegard (1098–1179) resolves thorny passages of Scripture, theological questions, and two issues in hagiographic texts—the lives of Saints Martin and Nicholas.[1] The *Solutions* joins Hildegard's *Homilies on the Gospels*, which were directed to her nuns, as evidence of Hildegard's exegetical writing as well as her authority as an exegete. We know of no other twelfth-century woman, and perhaps no other medieval woman, who wrote in standard genres of exegesis—homilies and *solutiones*—and whose interpretations of Scripture were sought by male audiences.[2] Hildegard composed the *Solutions* in response to repeated requests from Guibert of Gembloux (1124/25–1213) and the monks at Villers, probably during the years 1176 to 1179.[3] Guibert worked as Hildegard's secretary

---

[1] The translation is based on the text in J.-P. Migne's Patrologia Latina (PL 197:1037–54), but the Latin in the PL has been compared carefully and corrected in accordance with the principal manuscript of the *Solutiones*, Wiesbaden, Hessische Landesbibliothek 2 (*R*). The *Solutiones* are copied within the *Epistolae* (fols. 328ra–434ra), at 381rb–386ra. The corrected Latin text also agrees with the edition of the *Solutiones* by Christopher Evans, forthcoming from Corpus Christianorum, Continuatio Mediaevalis. I am grateful to Christopher Evans for providing a preprint copy of his edition. See below, 37–38, on the manuscripts and editions.

[2] For the Latin text of the *Homilies on the Gospels*, see *Expo. Euang.* For the translation, see *Homilies on the Gospels*. For a study of the homilies, see Kienzle, *Hildegard's Gospel Homilies*.

[3] On the *Solutiones*, see Kienzle, *Hildegard's Gospel Homilies*, 102–8; Anne Clark Bartlett, "Commentary, Polemic, and Prophecy in Hildegard of Bingen's

1

at Rupertsberg from 1177 to 1179 and remained there after her death until 1180. Hildegard had already sent some of her writings to Villers and Gembloux. The monks at Villers had received the *Book of Life's Merits* (*Liber vite meritorum*) by 1176, as had the community at Gembloux, and both were hearing it read in the refectory.[4]

Hildegard in the 1170s

By the 1170s Hildegard's visionary and exegetical authority was renowned. How did she attain this level of authority in the eyes of the male monastic communities who sought her exegetical knowledge? When did her talents become evident, and how did they develop? The gift for prophecy had apparently asserted itself at the age of five, when she foretold the coloring of a calf still in the womb.[5] Hildegard had been born in 1098

'Solutiones triginta octo quaestionum,'" *Viator* 23 (1992): 153–65; Bernard McGinn, "Hildegard of Bingen as Visionary and Exegete," in *Hildegard von Bingen in ihrem historischen Umfeld: internationaler wissenschaftlicher Kongress zum 900jährigen Jubiläum, 13.–19. September 1998, Bingen am Rhein*, ed. Alfred Haverkamp (Mainz: P. von Zabern, 2000), 333–34.

   [4] On the reception of the work, see Michael Embach, *Die Schriften Hildegards von Bingen. Studien zu ihrer Überlieferung und Rezeption im Mittelalter und in der Frühen Neuzeit*, Eruditi Sapientia 4 (Berlin: Academie Verlag, 2003), 120–24. See also Albert Derolez, "The Manuscript Transmission of Hildegard of Bingen's Writings: The State of the Problem," in *Hildegard of Bingen: The Context of Her Thought and Art*, ed. Charles Burnett and Peter Dronke (London: Warburg Institute, 1998), 21 and 28 on Dendermonde, Benedictine abbey, MS 9. *Vite mer.* xliv–xlvi; Guibert, *Epistolae* 23, 253, lines 56–61. See also *Letters* 2, 108a, 44–46, the text of which is not included in *Epistolarium* 2. See also *Letters* 2, 107, 43, where in 1176 the brothers of Villers acknowledged that they had received an unnamed work from the seer.

   [5] Bruno, priest of Saint Peter in Strasbourg, *Acta inquisitionis de virtutibus et miraculis S. Hildegardis*, ed. Petrus Bruder, *Analecta Bollandiana* 2 (1883): 124–25; Anna Silvas, trans. and annot., *Jutta and Hildegard: The Biographical Sources* (University Park: Pennsylvania State University Press, 1999), 267. On the canonization proceedings, see Barbara J. Newman, "Hildegard and

at Bermersheim (near Mainz) and was dedicated around eight years later to a religious life in the care of the holy woman Jutta. On All Saints' Day in 1112, Jutta and Hildegard were immured at the Benedictine monastery of Disibodenberg,[6] where a small women's community developed with Jutta as superior but in dependence on the abbot of Disibodenberg.[7] Upon Jutta's death in 1136, Hildegard became the *magistra*, that is, the superior and teacher of the community.[8]

About five years later, in 1141, Hildegard experienced a vision that instructed her to "speak and write" what she heard and saw.[9] With the permission of Abbot Kuno, Hildegard spent about a decade producing her first work, *Sciuias*. Already she expressed strong views about exegesis; in God's voice she criticized contemporary schoolmasters for neglecting patristic commentary, and she identified herself as the person who was called to revive and continue the teaching of the doctors.[10] A second work followed, the *Book of Life's Merits*, over which

---

Her Hagiographers: The Remaking of Female Sainthood," in *Gendered Voices: Medieval Saints and Their Interpreters*, ed. Catherine Mooney (Philadelphia: University of Pennsylvania Press, 1999), 16–34.

[6] Silvas, *Jutta and Hildegard*, 54, scrutinizes the evidence of these suppositions. See also John Van Engen, who notes the six years between Hildegard's oblation and her immurement at Disibodenberg and asserts that Hildegard "remained connected to her familial household in some way," in "Abbess: 'Mother and Teacher,'" in *Voice of the Living Light: Hildegard of Bingen and Her World*, ed. Barbara Newman (Berkeley: University of California Press, 1998), 32.

[7] See the letter of Guibert of Gembloux to Bovo in Silvas, *Jutta and Hildegard*, 109–11; Guibert, *Epistolae*, 2.38, 367–79.

[8] Guibert of Gembloux to Bovo, in Silvas, *Jutta and Hildegard*, 111; Guibert, *Epistolae*, 2.38, 375, lines 297–99.

[9] *Sciuias, Protestificatio (Preface)* p. 3, lines 18–21; *Scivias* (Eng.) 59. References to Hildegard's visionary works (*Sciuias, Vite mer., Diu. operum*) give the numbers for the part or vision, the chapter, and the page in that order, except for the prefaces, for which only pages are provided.

[10] *Sciuias* 3.18, 586, lines 379–91; *Scivias* (Eng.) 499.

she toiled from approximately 1158 to 1163;[11] a third, the *Book of Divine Works* (*Liber diuinorum operum*), was nearly finished in 1170 and probably completed in 1174.[12] In the meantime, Hildegard founded two communities for women: Rupertsberg, where she and her nuns settled around 1150, and then Eibingen in 1165. From approximately 1160 to 1170, she made trips to various monasteries and cathedrals in the Rhineland to deliver spiritual advice and exhortations, a series of journeys that have become known misleadingly as "preaching tours." While Hildegard can be said to have preached, probably in the venue of a chapter house, there are no grounds for concluding that she engaged in the sort of public tours that Bernard of Clairvaux (1090–1153) and other male ecclesiastical leaders undertook.[13]

Behind the composition of Hildegard's visionary treatises and numerous other works lay the profound insights that she experienced in her visions and took from her continuing study and exchange with monastic mentors, brothers, and sisters. Three decisive visions of 1141, 1163, and 1167 included an exegetical mandate. Hildegard reports that in 1141 she attained the sudden understanding of the spiritual sense of the Scriptures: "And suddenly I knew the meaning of the exposition [*intellectum expositionis*] of the Psalter, the Gospels, and other catholic books from the volumes of the Old as well as

---

[11] *Vite mer.* 9, lines 26–29. She acknowledges the same girl in the preface of the *Diu. operum* 46, lines 29–30: *testificante etiam eadem puella cuius in superioribus uisionibus mentionem feci.* See Preface, xi.

[12] Peter Dronke has identified Letter 217 as a cover letter for the codex. Dronke and Derolez believe that the manuscript in question is the uncorrected version of the oldest manuscript of the *Diu. operum* (Ghent University Library MS 241). It represents a direct copy from Hildegard's wax tablets and shows the modifications suggested by her collaborators and correctors (*Diu. operum* xii).

[13] See Kienzle, *Hildegard's Gospel Homilies*, 47–57. On Bernard's preaching tours, see Kienzle, *Cistercians, Heresy and Crusade (1145–1229): Preaching in the Lord's Vineyard* (Woodbridge, UK: Boydell and Brewer, 2001), 90–108.

the New Testaments."[14] The 1163 vision opened the way to understanding Genesis 1 and John 1; it shook her deeply and brought the onset of illness. A milder vision followed in 1167, enhancing her comprehension of the same texts and compelling her to write the *Book of Divine Works*.[15]

Hildegard was in frequent contact with bishops and archbishops as well as religious communities of Benedictines, Cistercians, and canons. A few examples among many will suffice here to illustrate her expansive network and high regard. Abbot Philip of Park, near Louvain, came to talk to Hildegard face to face in the early 1170s, and a twelfth-century copy of *Sciuias* was produced at that monastery.[16] Abbot Gottfried of Salem expressed his admiration after reading her visions, and an illuminated *Sciuias*

---

[14] *Sciuias, Protestificatio* 3–4, lines 24–33: *Factum est in millesimo centesimo quadragesimo primo Filii Dei Iesu Christi incarnationis anno, cum quadraginta duorum annorum septemque mensium essem, maximae coruscationis igneum lumen aperto caelo ueniens totum cerebrum meum transfudit et totum cor totumque pectus meum uelut flamma non tamen ardens sed calens ita inflammauit, ut sol rem aliquam calefacit super quam radios suos ponit. Et repente intellectum expositionis librorum, uidelicet psalterii, euangelii et aliorum catholicorum tam ueteris quam noui testamenti uoluminum sapiebam (Scivias* [Eng.] 59).

[15] Hildegard states in the Prologue that she was sixty-five years old (hence 1167) when she felt compelled to write down these visions, the first of which occurred in 1163, when she had just completed the *Vite mer.* (*Life of Hildegard,* 66–67). See *Diu. operum* 45, lines 5–14: *qui primus annus exordium presentium uisionum fuit, cum sexaginta quinque annorum essem, tanti misterii et fortitudinis uisionem uidi, ut tota contremiscerem et pre fragilitate corporis mei inde egrotare inciperem. Quam uisionem tandem per septem annos scribendo uix consummaui. Itaque in millesimo centesimo sexagesimo tercio Dominice incarnationis anno . . . uox de celo facta est ad me, dicens; V. Hild.* 2.16, 43, lines 1–10: *Subsequenti demum tempore mysticum et mirificam uisionem uidi, ita quod omnia uiscera mea concussa sunt et sensualitas corporis mei extincta est, quoniam scientia mea in alium modum conuersa est, quasi me nescirem. Et de Dei inspiratione in scientiam anime mee quasi gutte suauis pluuie spargebantur, quia et Spiritus Sanctus Iohannem euangelistam imbuit, cum de pectore Iesu profundissimam reuelationem suxit, ubi sensus ipsius sancta diuinitate ita tactus est, quod absconsa mysteria et opera aperuit, "In principio erat uerbum," et cetera.*

[16] Brussels, Royal Library, Cod. 11568 (1492). See Derolez, "Manuscript Transmission," 26, 28; *Sciuias* xliv–xlv; *Epistolarium* 2, 179R, 408–9; *Letters* 2, 179R, 142.

manuscript from the twelfth century takes its provenance, if not production, from the same Cistercian abbey of Salem.[17] Another early manuscript of *Sciuias*, now missing, has a provenance of the Cistercian abbey of Eberbach, whose Abbot Eberhard corresponded with Hildegard.[18] Ludwig, abbot of Saints Eucharius and Matthias in Trier,[19] assisted her with correcting the *Book of Divine Works* after her secretary Volmar's death in 1173.[20] The epilogue to the work attests that Ludwig himself assisted Hildegard (*per seipsum*) and procured aid for her through other learned men (*per alios sapientes*).[21] Yet another dimension of Hildegard's collaboration relates to the expansion of her exegetical mission in the 1160s and 1170s, when she allied with Ekbert and Elisabeth of Schönau to denounce the Cathars and their beliefs.

Writings from the last decade of Hildegard's life demonstrate the intellectual confidence that she had acquired. In the

[17] Heidelberg, Universitätsbibliothek, Cod. Sal. X, 16. See Derolez, "Manuscript Transmission," 26, 28. See *Sciuias* xxxix–xliii. The editors of this volume cite on xl–xli a passage in which G[ottfried] of Salem writes, *uidi et legi maxima sacramenta mysteriorum Dei, que per te in libro a te scripto Dominus scientiarum indignis hominibus aperiens reserauit* (Wiesbaden, Hess. LB, Hs, 2, f. 348rb; PL 197:285D). *Epistolarium* 2, 200, 453, lines 9–12; *Letters* 2, 200, 175.

[18] Former Collection, F. W. E. Roth; Derolez, "Manuscript Transmission," 26, 28; *Epistolarium* 1, 82, 184–85; *Letters* 1, 82, 179.

[19] *Epistolarium* 2, 215, 474; *Letters* 2, 215, 196–97. *Epistolarium* 2, 217, 476–78; *Letters* 2, 217, 198–99.

[20] See *Letters* 2, 214, 215, 215R, and 217, in *Epistolarium* 3, 471–78; *Letters* 3, 194–99. According to Dronke and Derolez, the *magistra* sent Ludwig what is now the Ghent manuscript of the *Diu. operum*, the oldest manuscript of the work. Ludwig would have corrected it and returned it to Hildegard for her final scrutiny. See Peter Dronke, *Women Writers of the Middle Ages: A Critical Study of Texts from Perpetua (d. 203) to Marguerite Porete (d. 1310)* (Cambridge and New York: University of Cambridge Press, 1984), 312–13. In *Diu. operum* lxxxvi–xcvi, Derolez examines the Ghent manuscript and identifies three correctors: Corrector 1 makes corrections as directed by Hildegard and introduces the commentary on the opening of Genesis; Corrector 2 corrects style and grammar; and Corrector 3, perhaps Guibert of Gembloux, makes limited changes and always cancels the text he amends.

[21] *Diu. operum, Epilogus* 464, lines 16–33.

1170s, Hildegard began organizing the writing of her *vita* and composed the *Life of Saint Disibod* and the *Explanation on the Athanasian Creed*, as well as the *Solutions*.[22] She boldly resisted the archbishop of Mainz when he ordered her to disinter an excommunicated man buried on her convent grounds. An interdict was imposed on her monastery between 1178 and 1179, and she responded with a powerful protest to the prelates at Mainz (Letter 23).[23] Hildegard proclaimed that God implanted the authorizing vision for the letter in her soul before her birth and explained that Adam's transgression resulted in the loss of the divine voice that he shared with the angels, but voices and instruments assist the soul's restoration to its heavenly condition. The community's song manifests the ability to hear the celestial symphony.[24] Therefore, Hildegard argues, the prelates who prohibit singing endanger their souls and disobey God's command for the elect to sing divine praises. Moreover, the interdict denied Hildegard and her sisters the Eucharist, which she considered necessary for cleansing them from sin and for sanctifying their bodies. Hildegard's voice resounds strongly

---

[22] *Two Hagiographies; Expl. Symb.*, in *Opera minora*, 109–33.

[23] *Epistolarium* 1, 23, 61–66; *Letters* 1, 23, 76–80. See the detailed study of Wolfgang Felix Schmitt, "Charisma gegen Recht? Der Konflikt der Hildegard von Bingen mit dem Mainzer Domkapitel 1178/79 in kirchenrechtsgeschicht-licher Perspektive," *Hildegard von Bingen 1098–1998, Binger Geschichtsblätter* 20 (1998): 124–59. On Hildegard and the archbishops of Mainz, see also John Van Engen, "Letters and the Public Persona of Hildegard," in *Hildegard von Bingen in ihrem historischen Umfeld: internationaler wissenschaftlicher Kongress zum 900jährigen Jubiläum, 13.–19. September 1998, Bingen am Rhein*, ed. Alfred Haverkamp (Mainz: P. von Zabern, 2000), 379–89; Sabina Flanagan, *Hildegard of Bingen, 1098–1179: A Visionary Life*, 2nd ed. (London and New York: Routledge, 1998), 17–18, 22–26.

[24] See Stephen D'Evelyn, "Heaven as Performance and Participation in the *Symphonia armonie celestium revelationum* of Hildegard of Bingen," in *Envisaging Heaven in the Middle Ages*, ed. Ad Putter and Carolyn A. Muessig, Routledge Studies in Medieval Religion and Culture (London and New York: Routledge, 2006), 155–65.

in this letter, perhaps her last, and Solution 21 echoes a theme from that well-known letter.

Hildegard's writings from the 1170s reveal a confident teacher who spoke from a broad comprehension of Scripture. The understanding of Genesis that Hildegard elaborated in the *Book of Divine Works* and other writings strengthened her confidence in her exegetical authority. She now wove the themes of salvation history together with the progress of human life and wisdom and her own process of aging. Hildegard's brilliant image of marrow describes fittingly how she had by then attained the fullness of confident wisdom that had begun over forty years earlier with the infusion of scriptural understanding into the marrow of her body and soul.

The *Solutions*

Given Hildegard's many undertakings in the 1170s, it is little wonder that Guibert of Gembloux was obliged to press her repeatedly for her responses. In Letter 105, dated to 1176, Guibert sent thirty-five questions on behalf of the monks at Villers, who avidly desired that Hildegard resolve various scriptural problems (*questiones . . . absoluendas*).[25] In Letter 106, also dated to 1176, Guibert again requests the solutions (*questionibus illis . . . ad te soluendas*) and persuasively describes the Holy Spirit's inspiration of Hildegard with the image of breezes that she may trust to fill her sails and guide her through the sea of problem solving (*mare solutionis*) to a calm port.[26] Hildegard's reply employs language that reflects the requested genre of writing (*aliquas solutiones*) and its function.[27] Letters

[25] Guibert, *Epistolae* 19, 238, lines 103–5: *Questiones autem ille, quas per me predicti reuerentissimi fratres sanctitati tue absoluendas transmittunt, in hunc modum se habent* (Hildegard, *Letters* 2, 105, 34–39).

[26] Guibert, *Epistolae* 20, 244, lines 12–23; Hildegard, *Letters* 2, 106, 39–40.

[27] Hildegard refers specifically to the genre in *Epistolarium* 2, 106R, *Epistolarium* 2, 67–68, lines 46–55: *De questionibus uero plus mihi soluendas misisti, ad*

107 and 108 ask Hildegard to address the monks' questions (*questiones*).[28] Another letter implores the community at Rupertsberg to press Hildegard to finish the solutions; the same letter acknowledges receipt of the *Book of Divine Merits*.[29] By the following year, she had made some progress, for in Letter 109 (1177), Guibert asks her to continue working on the solutions.[30] Finally, in Letter 109R, Hildegard states that she has been working on the solutions to his questions (*in solutionibus questionum uestrarum laboraui*), that she has completed fourteen solutions so far (*quattuordecim solutiones earundem questionum*), and that she will return to work on the others to the best of her ability and with God's help.[31] She does not, however, provide her complete solutions to his questions until sometime thereafter. Perhaps she completed them only when Guibert came to work at Rupertsberg and could press and assist her in person.[32]

---

uerum lumen prospexi, obsecrans ut de riuulo uiui fontis ad bibendum ab ipso mihi daretur, quatenus aliquas solutiones rescriberem, quamuis infirmitate corporis mei usque adhuc laborem, et a lacrimis necdum temperari ualeam, quoniam baculum consolationis mee non habeo, cum tamen magnum gaudium de anima ipsius habeam, quoniam de mercede eius secura sum. Et licet tanto, ut dixi, solatio destitute et disponendis monasterii nostri utilitatibus occupata sim, tamen, quantum per gratiam Dei possum, in prefatis questionibus enondandis laboro (*Letters* 2, 106R, 41).

[28] Guibert, *Epistolae* 21, 22, 246–47, 249–50; Hildegard, *Letters* 2, 107, 108, 42–44. The authorship of these letters is problematic, as is that of Guibert's Letter 23, which claims that 21 and 22 were written without his knowledge. See below, note 29, and Monika Klaes, "Vorbemerkungen zum zweiten Band," *Epistolarium* 2, 231–36.

[29] Guibert, *Epistolae* 23, 252–53; Hildegard, *Letters* 2, 108a, 44–46.

[30] Guibert, *Epistolae* 24, 255, lines 17–20: *Oro itaque te, o mater et domina, ut, quoad uiuis et sapis, cepto exsoluendarum questionum operi insistas, et pro innumeris excessibus <meis> commune Dominum iugiter interpellare non desistas* (*Letters* 2, 109, 47).

[31] *Epistolarium* 2, 109R, 271, lines 45–54, at line 48 and lines 51–52; *Letters* 2, 109R, 41.

[32] *Epistolarium* 2, 109R, 271, lines 45–53; *Letters* 2, 109R, 48–49. L. Van Acker discusses the complexities of dating and arranging the letters in "Einleitung," *Epistolarium* 1, vii–lxx. From the letters acknowledging the completion of fourteen solutions (Hildegard 109R and Guibert, *Epistolae* 2, 26), Sabina Flanagan

In the same letter (109R), Hildegard urges Guibert to heed Song of Songs 2:4-5: "The king brought me into the wine cellar and appointed charity within me. Make me steady with flowers, surround me with evils, because I languish with love."[33] She interprets the verse allegorically with a blend of the senses of Scripture: typology, the allegory of salvation history, a moral lesson for Guibert and the monks, and the anagogical contemplation of heaven. The king represents God, the wine cellar stands for the Old Law, and the flowers signify the Son of God, the Sun who illumined the world through his incarnation. Charity refers to the inextinguishable fire burning in the hearts of the faithful over history. They have been sustained by flowers of martyrdom and refreshed by the hope of eternal blessedness. They languish with eternal hunger and thirst for God's justice until they reach eternal life. Hildegard advises her audience that they have been marked by the same charity in order that they may reject the world out of love for God's son, who appointed charity in them.

Hildegard concludes with a paradoxical affirmation of her subordination to Guibert and the monks' authority. She says that she is subject to the teaching authority of their deep wisdom, but at the same time, their request has led her to look toward the true light and work on the answers to their questions. She clearly states that she is solving exegetical problems

---

seems to conclude that Hildegard did not complete the text: "Hildegard returned answers to only fourteen of them before she died, and for want of a better alternative, Guibert finally told the monks to direct their questions to one of the 'masters of France'" (Flanagan, *Hildegard*, 204). Guibert's Letter 26, found in *Epistolae* 2, 271–94, is highly complicated, and the tone of Guibert's defense of himself to Radulf, a monk of Villers, in the face of accusations about his familiarity with the nuns of Rupertsberg must be taken into account when evaluating this statement. Anna Silvas discusses Guibert's letters to and about Hildegard and the context for Letter 26 in *Jutta and Hildegard*, 90–94.

[33] *Vulg.: Introduxit me rex in cellam vinariam, et ordinauit in me caritatem. Fulcite me floribus, stipate me malis. Quia amore langueo.*

first upon request, second with God's inspiration, and third in subjection to male teaching authority. These three problem-solving circumstances entail three literary genres. Hildegard utters the explanatory statements in epistolary form, but they confirm the authorization of a second accepted literary genre: the *solutiones*.[34] The account of the vision itself constitutes a third literary genre, practiced by Hildegard in other writings as well. In terms of literary form, therefore, the visions that she reports in Letter 109R fall within and are subordinate to the two genres of the letter and the *solutio*; in a like manner Hildegard places her visionary authority within the bounds of male teaching authority at the same time that she claims authoritative interpretations through genres used nearly exclusively by men.

An exchange of letters, now numbered 106 and 106R, precedes the *Solutiones* in Wiesbaden, Hessische Landesbibliothek Manuscript 2 (the Riesenkodex). Hildegard asserts in Letters 106R and 109R that Guibert sent her questions to be resolved, that she looks to the true light and to the living fountain of wisdom, and that despite many travails she is writing *solutiones*.[35] Prefacing the text with a letter in the Riesenkodex may have served a threefold purpose, analogous to the three aforementioned problem-solving circumstances and the three corresponding literary genres. Examining why letters would precede the *Solutiones* or, alternatively, why the

[34] On the genre, see Beryl Smalley, *The Study of the Bible in the Middle Ages* (Oxford: Oxford University Press, 1952; repr. 1985), 66–82; Nikolaus M. Häring, "Commentary and Hermeneutics," in *Renaissance and Renewal in the Twelfth Century*, ed. Robert L. Benson and Giles Constable with Carol D. Lanham, Medieval Academy Reprints for Teaching (Toronto, Buffalo, and London: University of Toronto Press, 1991), 177, 182; Jean Châtillon, "La Bible dans les écoles du XIIe siècle," in *Le Moyen Age et la Bible*, ed. Pierre Riché and Guy Lobrichon, La Bible de tous les temps 4 (Paris: Beauchesne, 1984), 186–87; Bartlett, "Commentary, Polemic, and Prophecy," 154.

[35] *Epistolarium* 2, 106–106R, 265–68 at 267; *Letters* 2, 39–41 at 41; *Epistolarium* 2, 109R, 269–71 at 271, lines 45–53; *Letters* 2, 109R, 48–49 at 49.

Solutiones would be included within the collection of letters, leads to some important thoughts on Hildegard's authority as an exegete and the literary forms she chooses. Why would the *Solutiones* not stand alone as an independent group of texts within the Riesenkodex? Hildegard's Letter 109R recounts a vision and responds to Guibert's evocation of Hildegard's infusion with the Spirit (Letter 106). Their correspondence, therefore, first casts the work as inspired. The interpretations come from the "true light."

Second, the correspondence about the *Solutiones* situates Hildegard's work within the established genre of monastic letters, some of which were exchanged to probe exegetical or theological problems.[36] Within Hildegard's *oeuvre*, they join certain of Hildegard's letters that respond to complex questions that were being debated in the schools. Hildegard speaks in the role of *magistra* (teacher) when she writes about the Trinity in Letter 40R responding to Odo of Soissons and in Letter 31R to Eberhard of Bamberg.[37] She interprets Ezekiel's visions in Letter 84R: the animals seated around the throne of Yahweh, the tetramorph with the faces of a man, a lion, an eagle, and a

---

[36] See Beverly M. Kienzle, "New Introduction," in the revised edition of *The Letters of St. Bernard of Clairvaux*, trans. Bruno Scott James (Stroud, UK: Sutton, 1998), viii–xviii; Beverly Kienzle and Susan Shroff, "Cistercians and Heresy: Doctrinal Consultation in Some Twelfth-Century Correspondence from Southern France," *Cîteaux: Commentarii cistercienses* 41 (1990): 159–66; Beverly M. Kienzle, "The Works of Hugo Francigena: *Tractatus de conversione Pontii de Laracio et exordii Salvaniensis monasterii vera narratio; epistolae* (Dijon, Bibliothèque Municipale MS 611)," in *Sacris erudiri* 34 (1994): 281–82, 303–11; Giles Constable, *Letters and Letter Collections*, Typologie des sources du moyen âge 17 (Turnhout: Brepols, 1976).

[37] On the Trinity, see the correspondence with Odo of Soissons and with Eberhard of Bamberg: *Epistolarium* 1, 40–40R, 102–5; *Letters* 1, 40–40R, 109–12; *Epistolarium* 1, 31–31R, 82–88; *Letters* 1, 30–31R, 94–99. Bernard McGinn discusses these letters in "Hildegard of Bingen as Visionary and Exegete," 333–34. Anne Clark Bartlett highlights the tension between cloister and schools in "Commentary, Polemic, and Prophecy," 153–65.

bull, and the four wheels next to four cherubim each covered with eyes (Ezek 1:4-11, 28, 43; 10:1-10, 22; 11:22-23).[38] Hildegard comments on the meaning of the mountain of myrrh and incense (Song 4:6) in an intriguing short text edited with her letters and on Psalm 103:8 in a brief *sermo* (sermon). In the first of these, Hildegard speaks in the first person, seemingly in the voice of God, but her reference to daughters suggests that she is merging God's voice with her own: "I wish to cleanse the dense clouds among my daughters [*in filiabus meis*], because I do not want to be without them."[39] In the second text, she warns against the vice of pride.[40] Both of these seem to be notes that she could have developed or included in a longer work.

Hildegard is the only woman of her time, as far as we know, to author exegetical letters for men and their communities. Generally, women in monastic communities requested letters on scriptural questions from male teachers. The nuns at Admont corresponded with Gerhoh of Reichersberg to seek his interpretation of Psalm 50 and probably also that of the centurion in Matthew 8:5-13. Heloise sought Abelard's views on Scripture; his response is found in the *Problemata Heloissae*. Nonetheless, communities of women engaged in the exchange of letters, which involved some level of training in the *ars dictaminis*, the art of composing letters. While the best-known letters from individual learned women in the twelfth century are those of Heloise, Hildegard, and Elisabeth of Schönau,[41] less-renowned

---

[38] See Kienzle and Travis A. Stevens, "Intertextuality in Hildegard's Works: Ezekiel and the Claim to Prophetic Authority," in *A Companion to Hildegard of Bingen*, ed. Beverly Kienzle, Debra L. Stoudt, and George Ferzoco (Leiden: Brill, 2013), 137–62.

[39] See Kienzle, *Hildegard's Gospel Homilies*, 46, n. 108; 71. On Song 4:6, see *Epistolarium* 3, 380, 138–39; *Letters* 3, 380, 169–70.

[40] On Ps 103:8, see *Epistolarium* 3, 377, 133–34; *Letters* 3, 377, 169–70.

[41] See Constant J. Mews, *The Lost Love Letters of Heloise and Abelard: Perceptions of Dialogue in Twelfth-Century France*, trans. Neville Chiavaroli and Constant J. Mews (New York and Basingstoke, UK: Palgrave, 2001); Mews, *Abelard and*

women also composed and exchanged letters, including the religious women who wrote to Hildegard for advice.[42] Alison Beach has uncovered nineteen previously unknown letters from Admont that demonstrate at least a basic training in the *ars dictaminis* on the part of the nuns. She also points out a letter from a sister at Lippoldsberg who requested books on the *ars dictaminis* from the abbot of Reinhardsbrunn.[43] Current research on women's monasteries may reveal more evidence for the exchange of letters and familiarity with the art of letter writing.[44]

Thus the correspondence between Guibert and Hildegard establishes her work in two accepted genres: first the visionary account and second the monastic letter. In addition, the correspondence authorizes a third genre: the *solutiones*, a frequent vehicle for the thoughts of twelfth-century biblical scholars who grappled with Genesis and other passages of Scripture.[45] As a female exegete, Hildegard would perhaps not have ventured to compose a work in that scholastic genre if she had not been asked to do so. Hildegard's male correspondents follow established frameworks in their requests to her, as she does in

---

Heloise (Oxford and New York: Oxford University Press, 2005), 65, on the practice of *ars dictaminis* before the proliferation of manuals in the twelfth century, and 200–201. Elisabeth of Schönau, *The Complete Works*, trans. and intro. by Anne L. Clark (New York: Paulist Press, 2000), includes letters, notably at 142–47 for a well-known letter to Hildegard. This correspondence appears in *Epistolarium* 2, 201–3, 455–58, but Elisabeth's letters are not included.

[42] Among numerous examples, see *Epistolarium* 2, 159, 355; *Letters* 2, 159, 107; *Epistolarium* 2, 174, 395–96; *Letters* 2, 174, 134–36; *Epistolarium* 2, 250, 529; *Letters* 3, 250, 47.

[43] See Alison I. Beach, "Voices from a Distant Land: Fragments of a Twelfth-Century Nuns' Letter Collection," *Speculum* 77 (2002): 36 n. 13, on the letter from Lippoldsberg to Reinhardsbrunn.

[44] See Kienzle, *Hildegard's Gospel Homilies*, 71–72. See also *Letters of Peter Abelard: Beyond the Personal*, trans. Jan M. Ziolkowski (Washington, DC: The Catholic University of America Press, 2007), 53–60, and Mews, *Abelard and Heloise*, 65, on the practice of *ars dictaminis* before the proliferation of manuals in the twelfth century, and 200–201 on the *Problemata Heloissae*.

[45] On the genre, see above, note 34.

her responses, but the reversal of gender roles, with the female teacher or *magistra* providing the solutions to exegetical questions, remains striking.

What does Hildegard's reply to Guibert in the epistolary preface (Letter 106R) reveal about her exegesis? She opens with a vision of an allegory of Charity, as in Letter 109R, but now with a garden of virtues evoking Song 6:1. The garden's noblest flower blooms in Christ, just as the flower in Song 2:5 signifies Christ. Hildegard writes initially from a third-person point of view, describing the garden of Charity. She then unfolds the allegory in a straightforward manner, using explanatory verbs. The garden designates (*designat*) the holy virtues, and among the flowers, the lilies signify (*significant*) Mary's virginal nature.[46] After this brief direct explanation of the allegory, Hildegard turns to its moral application, reminding Guibert that nuns and monks who have renounced the world belong among the angelic orders. She subsequently applies the allegory personally to Guibert in a series of exhortations, urging him to remain in the valley of true humility, to gather the virtues from Charity's garden, and to gird on the sword of God's word and serve as a soldier of the true Solomon, clearly Christ. Finally, Hildegard moves to the anagogical plane as she beseeches the Holy Spirit to enkindle Guibert, that he may persevere unfailingly in service and merit in order to become a living stone of the heavenly Jerusalem.[47] Thus Letter 106R as well as the other letters exchanged with Guibert on the *Solutiones* set the stage for Hildegard to respond with an exegetical work that incorporates multiple senses of Scripture into a comprehensive interpretive guide to monastic spirituality and theology.

[46] PL 197:1039B reads *roses and other flowers* (*rosis et aliis*); PL 197:1039C reads *lilium significat*. *Epistolarium* 2, 106R, 265–68, at 266, lines 7–12; *Letters* 2, 40–41, at 40.

[47] *Epistolarium* 2, 106R, 265–68, at 266–67, lines 23–45; *Letters* 2, 106R, 40–41, at 41.

Content and Exegetical Method in the *Solutions*

Thirty-two of the thirty-eight questions that Hildegard addresses in the *Solutions* pertain directly to Scripture and touch on nineteen books of the Bible: Genesis, Exodus, First Kings, Second Kings, Third Kings (First Samuel), First and Second Chronicles, Psalms, Wisdom, Sirach, Job, Matthew, Luke, John, Acts, First and Second Corinthians, Ephesians, and Hebrews.[48] Hildegard adduces several other passages of Scripture in her responses. Two of the thirty-eight questions relate to the *vitae* of Saints Martin of Tours and Nicholas, and four questions probe theological and scriptural mysteries, such as Jesus' whereabouts after the crucifixion and before the ascension.

Six of the first seven questions deal with the creation story in Genesis. Question 1 asks how to reconcile the statement in Genesis 1 that God's work of creation lasted for six days with Sirach 18:1, which reads that God "created all things at the same time." The second question inquires whether the waters above the firmament (Gen 1:31) were material. Question 3 seeks to know if the humans in the resurrected spiritual body (1 Cor 15:44) will behold God through the corporeal eyes with which they saw God before the fall. The fourth query asks about the nature of God's speech and appearance in Genesis 2:16-17 and 3:6. Question 5 probes the meaning of God's statement that Adam became "one of us knowing good and evil" (Gen 3:22). The sixth query interrogates Hildegard on what sort of eyes, corporeal or spiritual, were opened for Adam and Eve before they sinned.

Hildegard resolves issues in Genesis according to a broad spiritual sense of Scripture; she explains the text in a straightforward manner with a view to clarifying the theological mean-

---

[48] The number of nineteen corrects the seventeen listed in Kienzle, *Hildegard's Gospel Homilies*, 103, which was based on the scriptural citations in the PL edition.

ing of the text. She does not expound the literal sense as it was taught in the schools, and she avoids approaches that probe the scientific plausibility of biblical events.[49] An interest in the historical sense of Scripture was increasingly evident in the twelfth-century schools, from Anselm of Laon (d. 1117) and the compilation of the *Glossa ordinaria* to the *Didascalion* of Hugh of Saint Victor (ca. 1096–1141) to the work of Peter Lombard (ca. 1096–1174), who gave the *Glossa ordinaria* canonical status when he cited it in his *Sententiae*. At around the same time that Hildegard was writing, Peter Comestor, chancellor of the cathedral school in Paris from 1168 to 1178, backed the usage of the *Glossa* as a fundamental tool for Parisian teachers and students, who disseminated it across Europe. His own *Historia scholastica* joined the *Glossa* as a basic reference work for the schools.[50]

A few examples from the *Glossa ordinaria* and the *Historia scholastica* will illustrate how Hildegard's approach differs. The *Glossa ordinaria* explains the literal meaning of segments of the text by means of an interlinear gloss and provides the broader allegorical and moral interpretations in the margins. Peter Comestor frequently grounds his discussion of the literal sense on the meanings of the biblical words in Hebrew and Greek in order to arrive at a clearer understanding of the Latin

[49] Bartlett, "Commentary, Polemic, and Prophecy," 161–64, describes this method as the "rhetoric of prophecy." Kienzle, "Hildegard of Bingen's Exegesis of Jesus' Miracles and the Twelfth-Century Study of Science," in *Delivering the Word: Preaching and Exegesis in the Western Christian Tradition*, ed. William John Lyons and Isabella Sandwell (London: Equinox Press, 2012), 99–119.

[50] Guy Lobrichon, "Une nouveauté: les gloses de la Bible," in *Le Moyen Age et la Bible*, ed. Pierre Riché and Guy Lobrichon, La Bible de tous les temps 4 (Paris: Beauchesne, 1984), 109–10. The adjective *ordinaria* entered common usage around 1220; by the mid-thirteenth century some commentators, such as Nicholas of Lyra, found the *Glossa ordinaria* out of date. Nevertheless, the *Sentences* of Peter Lombard and with them the *Glossa ordinaria* remained the basis for theological teaching until the sixteenth century (Lobrichon, "Une nouveauté," 101–2).

words. Moreover, the Greek often leads him to the opinions of Plato and Aristotle that he finds false.[51] Hildegard does not separate the units of her interpretation in the *Solutions* by spatial or exegetical categories (interlinear, marginal, allegorical, moral, and so on); nor does she do so in the *Homilies on the Gospels*. Instead, she constructs parallel narratives. The interlinear and marginal comments merge with the biblical text.[52]

Hildegard's Solution 6 provides an interesting case for comparison. She comments on Genesis 3:6, "The woman saw the tree," and distinguishes between spiritual and carnal vision, before and after the Fall. She refers briefly to carnal desires, while Peter Comestor interprets the vision after the fall as concupiscence and dwells on the notion of lust: Adam and Eve were like prepubescent children before they sinned.[53] The interlinear gloss explains the serpent's preceding temptation of Eve (Gen 3:4-5), namely, that the serpent wants to close the eyes of their hearts in order to open their carnal eyes. For the woman, the interlinear gloss observes, "Being carnal, women are seduced more easily."[54] The statement about carnal eyes and the eyes of the heart captures a theme of patristic exegesis, echoed by the marginal glosses on the same page. Hildegard develops this thesis in her own way in Solution 6, distinguishing between categories of vision corporeal and spiritual. Not surprisingly, however, the *magistra* does not repeat the comment on women;

[51] See, among many examples, Peter Comestor, *Scolastica Historia: Liber Genesis*, ed. Agneta Silwan, CCCM 191 (Turnhout: Brepols, 2005), 7, lines 20–24: *Hebreus habet* eloym, *quod tam singulare quam plurale est, id est* Deus *uel* dii, *quia tres persone unus Deus Creator est. Cum uero dixit Moyses*: creauit, *trium errores elidit: Platonis, Aristotilis, Epicuri.*

[52] See Kienzle, *Hildegard's Gospel Homilies*, 115–30.

[53] Peter Comestor, *Scolastica Historia* 41, lines 13–18: *Sed oculis eorum dicimus concupiscentiam et cognitionem eius. Erant enim in eis naturales motus concupiscentie, sed repressi et clausi ut in pueris usque ad pubertatem, et tunc tanquam riuuli aperti sunt et ceperunt moueri et diffundi. Quos cum prius in se esse non sensissent, tunc experti sunt et cognouerunt eos.*

[54] *Glossa ordinaria* 1.27.

in fact, she generally tends to emphasize Adam's sin more than Eve's in the *Solutions* and in the *Homilies*.[55]

Another example illustrates more subtle differences when all three texts attempt to explain the division of the waters in Genesis 1:7 and the distinction between the upper and the lower waters. The interlinear gloss clarifies terms with notations of "higher waters" and "denser waters"; it associates the higher waters with the angels and the lower waters with humans. The marginal glosses offer several interpretations from Augustine, one of which includes the distinction between angels and humans and interprets higher and lower as spiritual and carnal.[56] Peter Comestor probes more deeply into the nature of the waters, describing their firmness with the designations of *frozen* and *crystal*; he introduces Greek words; and he sees the firmament as the end of the lower waters while the higher waters are held above the earth and serve as the source for summer dewdrops.[57] In Solution 2, Hildegard

---

[55] Hildegard discusses Adam's (not Eve's) transgression at several points in the *Homilies on the Gospels*, particularly 1.30–33; 9.55–61, at 60–61; 22.100–104, at 102; 24.109–13, at 110; and 39.158–61, where she speaks in Adam's voice giving commands to creation. See Solution 8 below, 51, where Hildegard refers to the devil's seducing Eve. PL 197:1043C reads *etiam* instead of *Euam*, so this reference to Eve has not been noted.

[56] *Glossa ordinaria* 1.11.

[57] Peter Comestor, *Scolastica Historia* 11, lines 4–6 and 8–17; 12, lines 25–30: *Fecit ergo ea die Deus firmamentum in medio aquarum, id est quandam exteriorem mundi superficiem ex aquis congelatis, ad instar crystalli consolidatam et perlucidam. . . . Et dicitur firmamentum, non tantum propter sui soliditatem sed quia terminus est aquarum que super ipsum sunt, firmum et intransgressibile. Dicitur etiam celum, quia celat, id est tegit omnia inuisibilia uel sensibilia. Et cum legitur firmamentum celi, endiadis est, id est firmamentum quod est celum, ut cum dicitur creatura salis. Vnde et pro sui concameratione Grece dicitur uranon, id est palatum uel palates. Vel dicitur celum quasi casa elios, quia sol sub ipso positus ipsum illustrat. Hanc tamen circumuolutam concamerationem philosophus summitatem ignis intellexit. . . . Sane firmamentum diuidit aquas que sub ipso sunt ab aquis que super ipsum sunt. De quibus dicitur: Qui tegis aquis superiora eius. Et sunt sicut et ipsum congelate ut cristallus, ne igni solui possint, uel in modum nebule*

affirms the existence of material waters and differentiates the upper and lower waters with an explanation related to the role of the elements in the universe. Where the *Glossa* employs the term *densior* ("denser") for the lower waters, Hildegard describes them similarly as *grossiores* ("thicker" or "denser") and thereby able to reflect the heavenly bodies. Her major point, however, resides in her articulation of the functions or duties for which God created the two waters. The latter is a salient theme of her commentary on Genesis in the *Homilies*.[58] Again Hildegard's emphasis is theological, and the distance in content between Hildegard and the *Glossa*, whose texts reflect the patristic tradition, is less than that between Hildegard and Peter Comestor. Comestor's work includes the many additional sources that were being read in the schools.[59]

An overview of the remaining *Solutions* elucidates Hildegard's exegetical range and methods. After the six opening questions on Genesis, she turns to some texts that involve the patriarchs: Noah (Question 7), Abraham (Questions 8 and 9), Enoch and Elijah (Question 29). Hildegard offers a spiritual interpretation for the meaning of the bodies of angels (Question 8) and then gives a typological reading on the significance of why Abraham and Jacob made an oath by placing a hand under the thigh (Question 9 on Gen 24:1-3, 9; 47:29-30)[60] and for the meaning of the twofold cave (Question 10 on Gen 23:9).

---

esse uaporabiles. Cur vero ibi sint Deus nouit, nisi quod quidam autumant inde rorem descendere in estate.

[58] *Solution* 6, below, 47; *Solutiones* 6, PL 198:1041A: *Aquae vero inferiores istae de sub firmamento grossiores, speculum sunt coelestium luminarium*; Hildegard discusses the duties (*officia*) of various orders of creation in *Homilies on the Gospels* 1.30–33, 22.101–4. In Homily 22 she particularly expounds the duties of flying creatures and herds.

[59] Agneta Silwan, ed., "Introduction," in Peter Comestor, *Scolastica Historia*, xix–xxix.

[60] *Solutions* 1–6, 39–47; *Solutiones* 1–6, PL 197:1040B–1042, on the creation story. *Solutions* 8–10, 50–53; *Solutiones* 8–10, PL 197:1042C–1043D, on the patriarchs.

A group of questions connects the Old and New Testaments and explains typological interpretations: Question 11 links the fire in the burning bush and on Mount Sinai (Exod 3:2; 19:18) to the tongues of fire above the disciples at Pentecost (Acts 2:3); Question 12 asks Hildegard how to reconcile seemingly contradictory passages referring to the ark of the covenant in 1 Kings 8:9 and Hebrews 9:2-4.[61]

Question 31 probes the origin of evil thoughts, whether from the human heart (Matt 15:18-19) or from wicked angels (Ps 77:49). On the other hand, Question 13 queries Hildegard on the medium of Endor (1 Sam 28:7-25), as well as on Saul and Samuel (1 Chr 10:13). Hildegard relates the sin of Saul to that of Adam.

Several questions interrogate Pauline texts. Hildegard interprets the "tongues of angels" (Question 14 on 1 Cor 13:1), and the four dimensions—length, breadth, height, and depth (Question 15 on Eph 3:18)—as well as Paul's reference to being in the depth of the sea (Question 17 on 2 Cor 11:25) and his claim to be the least of the apostles (Question 18 on 1 Cor 15:9). In addition, she explains the sin of fornication (Question 19 on 1 Cor 6:18), the third heaven and the nature of prophecy (Question 24 on 2 Cor 12:2-4), and finally, the perception of corporeal and spiritual eyes (Question 32 on 2 Cor 4:18).

Hildegard's Solution 24 on the third heaven (2 Cor 12:2-4), a passage fundamental to understanding and shaping Christian mysticism, recalls the twelfth book of Augustine of Hippo's *Literal Commentary on Genesis*, which is devoted to this Pauline text, as well as Gregory the Great's treatment of Paul in the *Moralia in Iob*. Among the topics that Augustine and Hildegard discuss are the experience of seeing and experiencing in dreams (12.2), the ecstatic vision of the soul (12.2), and the difference between corporeal and spiritual vision (12.12).[62] Augustine's

---

[61] *Solutions* 12, 55; *Solutiones* 12, PL 197:1044BC.

[62] Augustine of Hippo, *De Genesi ad litteram libri duodecim*, ed. Joseph Zycha (Vienna: F. Tempsky, 1894), 12.2, 380–82; 12.12, 395–97.

commentary is perhaps best known for the three types of vision he distinguishes—corporeal, spiritual, intellectual—and Hildegard's knowledge of this distinction is apparent in her works.[63] Gregory explains Paul's access to hidden secrets alongside the apostle's physical suffering and humility as well as the limits on human knowing.[64] The Pauline text and the commentary by both Augustine and Gregory are the most influential texts for the development of Christian mysticism.[65] Furthermore, Hildegard alludes to John Scotus Eriugena's comparison of Paul to the eagle, John the Evangelist, who soared to heights that Paul could not attain.[66] Thus Hildegard deserves recognition as a commentator on Paul, not just as an exegete, but as one who shared mystical experience.

Another several questions address theological problems rather than immediate scriptural texts. Question 20 asks where the Lord was between the days of his resurrection and the event

[63] Kienzle, *Hildegard's Gospel Homilies*, 6–11; "Hildegard of Bingen," in *The Oxford Guide to the Historical Reception of Augustine*, ed. Karla Pollman and Willemien Otten, vol. 3 (Oxford: Oxford University Press, 2013), 652–55.

[64] Gregory the Great, *Moralia in Iob*, ed. Marcus Adriaen, CCSL 143, 143A, and 143B (Turnhout: Brepols, 1979–85), 8.29, 420, lines 31–35; 10.10, 550, lines 30–34; 12.2, 629, lines 32–34; 17.26, 871, lines 28–31; 18.7, 893, lines 20–26; 19.6, 963–64, lines 56–62, 73–85; 20.3, 1008, lines 105–15; and 31.51, 1621, lines 62–74.

[65] On Paul and Augustine, see Bernard McGinn, *The Presence of God: A History of Western Christian Mysticism*, vol. 1, *The Foundations of Mysticism: Origins to the Fifth Century* (New York: Crossroad, 1997), esp. 4, 70, 112, 206, and 254; on Gregory the Great, see Bernard McGinn, *The Presence of God: A History of Western Christian Mysticism*, vol. 2, *The Growth of Mysticism: Gregory the Great through the Twelfth Century* (New York: Crossroad, 1996), esp. 34–79; for McGinn's discussion of Hildegard's mystical experience, see McGinn, *Growth*, 333–36.

[66] This seems to be an echo of John Scotus Eriugena's evocation of John the Evangelist as an eagle in his homily on the prologue to the Gospel of John. See Iohannes Scotus, *Homélie sur le prologue de Jean*, ed. E. Jeauneau, SCh 151 (Paris: Les Éditions du Cerf, 1969), 1.201–9, and his comparison of John and Paul in 4.218–21. See Kienzle, *Hildegard's Gospel Homilies*, 11, 35, and 42, on Hildegard and John the Evangelist, and 91–92, 202, 274, and 277, on Hildegard and Eriugena.

of his ascension. The twenty-second question queries how souls acquire original sin. Question 25 focuses on grace and free will. The thirty-third question interrogates the nature of the fire in hell.[67] Question 34 poses the problem of whether saints in heaven and the wicked in hell know what things happen on earth.

Finally, Questions 37 and 38 address issues about saints' lives. The thirty-seventh question focuses on Martin of Tours. The thirty-eighth concerns the life of Saint Nicholas, but it also turns to Saints Peter and Paul.

Many questions phrase their inquiry with straight-forward interrogative words, such as: *quid est quod* ("Why is it that . . ."), *quomodo* ("How"), *cur, quare,* and forms of *qualis* ("what sort" or "of what sort"). These recall the methods of the schools as well as the playful monastic practice of riddles on Scripture, the *joca monachorum.*[68]

Certain questions lead Hildegard to a particular mode of interpretation, as when an allegorical explanation is sought for the length, breadth, height, and depth referred to in Ephesians 3:18 (Question 15).[69] In Question 19, Hildegard extracts both a moral and a physiological lesson from her explanation: the

---

[67] *Solutions* 33, 83; *Solutiones* 33, PL 197:1051C–1052A.

[68] Examples of each follow: *Quomodo: Solutions* 1, 39–40; *Solutiones* 1, PL 197:1040B. *Quid: Solutions* 2, 41–42; *Solutiones* 2, PL 197:1040D. *Quo genere: Solutions* 4, 44; *Solutiones* 4, PL 197:1041CD. *Quid est: Solutions* 5, 45–46; *Solutiones* 5, PL 197:1041D–1042A. *Quales: Solutions* 6, 47; *Solutiones* 6, PL 197:1042B. *Cur: Solutions* 9, 52; *Solutiones* 9, PL 197:1043C. *Quare: Solutions* 10, 53; *Solutiones* 10, PL 197:1043D–1044A. Other instances of the same words occur. This type of questioning reflects the attention to Genesis in the schools. It is interesting to compare the questions with the *joca monachorum,* the game-like questions and answers about Scripture that circulated widely in monastic circles. The latter tend to ask for recall of information, although they incorporate some interpretation, as in *Qui est mortuus et non natus? Adam.* See Jacques Dubois, "Comment les moines du Moyen Age chantaient et goûtaient les Saintes Ecritures," in *Le Moyen Age et la Bible,* ed. Pierre Riché and Guy Lobrichon, La Bible de tous les temps 4 (Paris: Beauchesne, 1984), 264–70. The questions posed in the *Solutions* ask for interpretation but not causal or scientific explanations.

[69] *Solutions* 15, 59–60; *Solutiones* 15, PL 197:1045BC.

devil sows discord and motivates sin from outside the body
(1 Cor 6:18), and from one human against another, but when
desire boils up in the veins and marrow, humans incite and
harm themselves within the body.[70]

This explanation corresponds to material in *Cause et Cure*
(*Causes and Cures*).[71] Laurence Moulinier, in her fine edition of
Cause et Cure and her learned introduction, signals parallels
between the *Causes* and the *Solutions*. Some of those extend to
the *Book of Divine Works* as well. Moulinier notes that the *Book
of Divine Works* incorporates the elements and humors into a
spiritual message with an exegetical perspective.[72]

While some of the *Solutions* treat the same material as the
Causes and the *Book of Divine Works*, they do so in a clearly exegetical genre.[73] The coincidence of content and the dating of the
works to Hildegard's last decade argue for viewing the three
works, or at least parts of them, together. Hildegard reflects
on elements and humors, macrocosm and microcosm, in three
genres: visionary accounts, expository notes, and the exegetical
commentary of the solution.

Two further *Solutions* demonstrate the interrelatedness of
Hildegard's works. Two questions address gospel pericopes
that Hildegard exegetes in the *Homilies on the Gospels*: Matthew
4:11 (the ministry of the angels to Jesus in the wilderness) and

---

[70] *Solutions* 19, 64; *Solutiones* 19, PL 197:1046BC.

[71] On marrow and lust, see *Cause* 2.143, 105; 1.26; 2.151, 114, lines 11–14;
2.284, 177, 1.14; 2.287, 179, lines 26–27, et al. Some examples are found in
Hildegard of Bingen on Natural Philosophy and Medicine, trans. Margret Berger
(Cambridge, UK: D. S. Brewer, 1999), 55.

[72] *Cause*, LIX–LXIII; Laurence Moulinier, "Abbesse et agronome: Hildegarde
et le savoir botanique de son temps," in *Hildegard of Bingen: The Context of Her
Thought and Art*, ed. Charles Burnett and Peter Dronke (London: Warburg
Institute, 1998), 135–56.

[73] See the notes to the translation below at *Solutions* 1, 39; 2, 41–42; 8, 50–51;
19, 64; 22, 67–68; 24, 71–73; 27, 76; and 30, 79–80. This is not an exhaustive list;
much more work is needed on the interrelatedness of Hildegard's various
works.

Luke 16:22-24 (the death and afterlife of the beggar Lazarus and the rich man). Question 21 inquires what sort of ministry the angels provided to Christ in the wilderness. Hildegard sets the context for the question in the gospel passage, when the devil left Jesus after his failure to tempt him. She then answers that the angels' ministry was to sound forth praises, because humankind overcame the devil's temptations through Christ.[74] This explanation corresponds in part to the interpretation she gives in one of the *Homilies* that the angels ministered to Jesus "in celestial harmony and praise, since they will praise God without end."[75] The two commentaries in both the *Solutions* and the *Homilies* connect the angels' ministry with their singing of praises.

The role of angels singing praises may evoke the song of Hildegard's sisters, elevating their voices to the level of the angelic.[76] Hildegard discusses the need and the theology for praising God in her well-known 1178 Letter 23 to the prelates at Mainz.[77] Her community had been placed under interdict because she had buried a man at Rupertsberg against the will of the Mainz clergy, so here she rebukes the prelates for prohibiting the nuns from praising God. She incorporates this reproach into an account of salvation history presented from the perspective of voices: the singing of Adam with the angels before the Fall, the voices of the prophets, the devil's efforts to suppress divine praise, the prelates' interdict on her church's singing praises to God, and the music of the nuns, which rejoins that of the angels. Thus the *Solutions*, which were probably completed during her last three years, and in particular Solution 21, share the common

---

[74] *Solutions* 21, 66; *Solutiones* 19, PL 197:1046D–1047A.

[75] *Homilies on the Gospels* 25, 116; *Expo. Euang.* 25, 260, lines 80–82.

[76] *Glossa* 4, 15 reads that "the retinue of angels teaches the glorious reward after our struggle" (*sicut in hoc agone militia nostra prestruitur, ita in obsequio angelorum gloriosa remuneratio docetur*).

[77] *Epistolarium* 1, 23, 61–66. *Letters* 1, 23, 76–80.

theme of singing with the homily on Matthew 4:11 and with
Letter 23, composed in 1178 near the end of Hildegard's life.
The salvific activity of singing, in which angels and humans
and notably Hildegard's own sisters partake, participates in
the course of salvation history as humans rise from the Fall
and attain eternal life. Furthermore, Hildegard warns that anyone, clearly any prelate, who imposes silence on a church and
prohibits singing God's praises will lose his place among the
chorus of angels.[78]

Question 36 probes another text that Hildegard explains
in her *Homilies on the Gospels*: the parable of Lazarus and the
rich man. The monks ask about the significance of the bosom
of Abraham, the finger of Lazarus, and the tongue of the rich
man (Luke 16:22-24). In Solution 36, Hildegard the teacher
(*magistra*) explains the bosom of Abraham allegorically as the
obedience showed to God, the finger of Lazarus as the ministry of obedience, and the rich man's tongue as self-will.[79] In
the two *Homilies* on the passage (37, 38), Hildegard develops
a moral interpretation different from her allegory in this solution. In the first text Abraham's bosom represents the comprehension and joyous embrace of the gospels and prophets for
all who fulfill them in deed (Homily 37) and, in the second
(Homily 38), the appetite for hope. Lazarus's finger denotes
in one homily (Homily 37) the smallest part of a deed dipped
in wisdom and, in the other (Homily 38), the tiniest matter
(*causae*) of one moaning for God. The rich man's tongue stands
for his excessive speech (Homily 37) and then (Homily 38)
for the works that he performed with the tongue. Hence her
readings are allegorical in Homily 37 and moral in Homily
38. The interpretation in Homily 38 more closely approaches

---

[78] *Epistolarium* 1, 23, 61–66; *Letters* 1, 23, 76–80.
[79] *Solutions* 36, 86; *Solutiones* 36, PL 197:1052CD.

Hildegard's exegesis in Solution 36, where the wealthy man himself designates pleasure and overindulges in sin and vice.[80]

Nonetheless, *solutiones* on Matthew 4:11 and Luke 16:22-24 do not simply repeat what Hildegard states in the *Homilies*.[81] Instead, in the two works she provides different and primarily tropological readings. This range of interpretation testifies to the depth of her exegetical knowledge and at the same time to her preference for tropological interpretation.

The Moral Interpretation of Scripture

Why did Hildegard prefer moral interpretation over the other senses of Scripture? Her response to Question 35 provides an extraordinary explanation of her thought on exegesis and moral teaching. The monks inquire why Jesus used parables. She replies that Jesus set forth parables to demonstrate that virtues can vanquish the spiritual vices.[82] She echoes the merit and even the necessity of teaching by parables in Letters 268 and 389. Drawing on the motif of new wine and old wineskins, Hildegard explains that the best wine in the skins signifies the sweetest doctrine, which Jesus taught people by means

---

[80] *Homilies on the Gospels* 38, 154: "'*A certain man*,' namely, Pleasure in the human being, '*was very rich*,' in the vicissitudes of the fatness of self will, '*and he wore purple and fine linen*,' that is, he entered into the appetite for sin through pleasures. '*And he feasted sumptously every day*,' namely, he increased every vice whatsoever before the face of his heart"; *Expo. Euang.* 38, 293, lines 1–3: "Homo quidam, *scilicet uoluptas in homine*, erat diues *ualde in uicissitudine pinguedinis propriae uoluntatis, et induebatur, id est iniit*, purpura, *scilicet gustum peccati*, et bisso, *uidelicet deliciis*, et epulabatur, *multiplicat cottidie unumquodque uicium*, splendide, *ante faciem cordis sui*."

[81] Hildegard does not echo the *Glossa ordinaria* here or anywhere that I have found. The *Glossa ordinaria* reflects Augustine's interpretation in *De Genesi ad litteram libri duodecim* 12.33, 429, lines 5–6: *in sinu eius, hoc est in secreto quietis eius (pauperis)*. Glossa 4, 139: *Sinus Abrahae est requies beatorum pauperum; Sinus Abrahae requies est patris in quae recumbunt venientes ab oriente et occidente cum Abraham, Ysaac, et Iacob.*

[82] *Solutions* 35, 85; *Solutiones* 35, PL 197:1052C.

of parables. Parables prove necessary because the serpent caused humans to lose their spiritual vision. Consequently, the divine mysteries are not to be seen except as one sees one's face in a mirror: "Those conceived in sin cannot grasp words of life other than in parables."[83] Furthermore, Hildegard the teacher (*magistra*) explains God's method of pedagogy, that "God set parables and metaphors before humankind, through which, usually, they are taught the way to salvation better than through the naked words themselves."[84]

These passages from the *Solutions* and the *Letters* recall Augustine's observation in *On Christian Doctrine* that "things are perceived more readily through similitudes."[85] Likewise, Hildegard's German predecessor Otloh of Saint Emmeram

[83] On the loss of spiritual vision, see *Solutions* 3, 6, and 8, 43, 47, 50–51; *Solutiones* 3, 6, and 8, PL 197:1041, 1042–43. *Epistolarium* 3, 389, 162, lines 326–33: *Botrorum autem optimum uinum suam dulcissimam doctrinam significat, qua homines in parabolis docebat, quia diuina mysteria generi per consilium serpentis obnubilato uidenda non sunt, nisi ut facies hominis in speculo, in quo tamen non est, resplendet. Quomodo enim posset uita a mortali homine uideri? Ipse enim obscura uerba hominibus locutus est, scilicet parabolas, quia in peccatis concepti uerba uitae aliter capere non possunt* (*Letters* 3, 389, 182–93, at 190).

[84] *Epistolarium* 3, 268, 18–19, at 18, lines 6–9: *Deus siquidem ab initio hominibus proposuit parabolas et similitudines, per quas plerumque couenientius quam nudis uerbis ad salute instruuntur* (*Letters* 3, 268, 63–64). Barbara J. Newman, *Sister of Wisdom: St. Hildegard of Bingen's Theology of the Feminine, with a New Preface, Bibliography, and Discography* (Berkeley and Los Angeles: University of California Press, 1997), 79–85, signals Hildegard's use of parables, *qua* personification of virtues, notably in her *Letters* 93, 23, 135, and 144, and the taste for personification of virtues in certain writings of Bernard of Clairvaux, Hugh of Saint Victor, and Rupert of Deutz.

[85] The exegete prepares himself to interpret signs, natural and conventional, knowing that "things are perceived more readily through similitudes," in Augustine of Hippo, *De doctrina christiana*, ed. J. Martin, CCSL 32 (Turnhout: Brepols, 1962), 2.6.6, 37, lines 15–23: *Nunc tamen nemo ambigit et per similitudines libentius quaeque cognosci et cum aliqua difficultate quaesita multo gratius inueniri . . . magnifice igitur et salubriter spiritus sanctus ita scripturas sanctas modificauit, ut locis apertioribus fami occurreret, obscurioribus autem fastidia detergeret.* On Augustine's interpretation of Scripture, see *Augustine and the Bible*, ed. and trans. Pamela Bright (Notre Dame, IN: University of Notre Dame Press, 1999).

(ca. 1010–ca. 1070) advocated teaching as Christ did, using gospel parables to illustrate how to combat vices and practice virtues.[86] Furthermore, Hildegard's statements on teaching with parables explain the value and method of the tropological interpretation implemented in her *Homilies on the Gospels*: she constructed parables of virtue and vice for the benefit of her community and created mirrors for biblical texts in order to elucidate their mysteries. Many of Hildegard's homilies set forth lessons of virtues combating vices in a dramatic struggle that recalls the plot of the *Ordo uirtutum*, her morality play.[87]

What do Hildegard's other works reveal about her use of the senses of Scripture? She employs threefold exegesis for some parts of the *Liber diuinorum operum*, which may stem from her familiarity with Gregory the Great, in particular his *Moralia in Iob*. In Gregory's famous prefatory letter to Leander of Seville, he describes the exegetical process with imagery of building, establishing the literal sense as foundation, the typological (*typica*) as structure, and the tropological as decoration.[88] Gregory put his exegetical principles into practice in the *Forty Homilies*

---

[86] See Kienzle, *Hildegard's Gospel Homilies*, 27–29. Otloh of Saint Emmeram, *Liber de admonitione clericorum et laicorum*, PL 146:255–64, at 252–54. See also the *Liber visionum*, ed. Paul Gerhardt Schmidt, Monumenta Germaniae Historia, *Quellen zur Geistesgeschichte des Mittelalters* 13 (Weimar: Herman Böhlaus Nachfolger, 1989), 33–34. On the *Liber visionum* in the context of monastic reform, see Ellen Joyce, "Speaking of Spiritual Matters: Visions and the Rhetoric of Reform in the *Liber visionum* of Otloh of St Emmeram," in *Manuscripts and Monastic Culture: Reform and Renewal in Twelfth-Century Germany*, ed. Alison I. Beach, Medieval Church Studies 13 (Turnhout: Brepols, 2007), 69–98.

[87] See Kienzle, *Hildegard's Gospel Homilies*, 199–243.

[88] Gregory the Great, *Moralia in Iob*, ed. Marcus Adriaen, *Ad Leandrum* 3, p. 4, lines 106–14, CCSL 143 (Turnhout: Brepols, 1979): *Sciendum uero est, quod quaedam historica expositione transcurrimus et per allegoriam quaedam typica inuestigatione perscrutamur, quaedam per sola allegoricae moralitatis instrumenta discutimus, nonnulla autem per cuncta simul sollicitius exquirentes tripliciter indagamus. Nam primum quidem fundamenta historiae ponimus; deinde per significationem typicam in arcem fidei fabricam mentis erigimus; ad extremum quoque per moralitatis gratiam, quasi superducto aedificum colore uestimus.* McGinn also

on the Gospels. In Homily 40, Gregory explains that the fruit of allegory is picked more sweetly when the truth of history solidly roots it. He also advises that he will explain the moral meaning of the text last, so that his listeners will better recall what they heard most recently.[89] Gregory strongly influenced monastic culture, and it should be no surprise that he would have inspired Hildegard's exegesis. The tropological character of her interpretation finds long-standing roots in the exegesis of Gregory the Great and its impact in monastic circles.[90]

Hildegard's Voice

Hildegard explains in the *Solutions* the preference for moral interpretation that she demonstrates in the *Homilies on the Gospels*, where she reveals a remarkable talent for combining drama and narrative. Is the voice of Hildegard evident in a similar way in the *Solutions*? Does she here employ varying modes of discourse, as she does in the *Homilies*? In the latter texts, Hildegard speaks in at least three modes. At times, she stands apart from the scriptural text and speaks in the third person with what I call the *vox expositricis.* More often, she tells a moral story in parallel to the gospel narrative, which I call her *vox narrativa.* In certain cases, she takes the voice of characters in the biblical passages she expounds. I call this voice the *vox dramatis personae.* She extends with her own words what the

---

notes the similarity between Gregory's method and Hildegard's in the *Diu. operum* in "Visionary and Exegete," 348.

[89] Gregory the Great, *Homeliae in euangelia*, ed. R. Étaix, CCSL 141 (Turnhout: Brepols, 1999), 40, 394, lines 9–12: *et quod uobis de moralitate historiae ualde est necessarium, hoc in expositionis nostrae ordine seruetur extremum, quia ea plerumque solent melius recoli que contingit postmodum audiri* (Gregory the Great, *Forty Gospel Homilies*, trans. David Hurst [Kalamazoo, MI: Cistercian Publications, 1990], 40, 371). See Stephen L. Wailes, *Medieval Allegories of Jesus' Parables* (Berkeley, Los Angeles, and London: University of California Press, 1987), 257.

[90] See Kienzle, *Hildegard's Gospel Homilies*, especially 55, 102, 123–24, 126–27.

biblical character says. She expands the words of God, Jesus, Adam, the older brother in the parable of the prodigal son, and other biblical speakers.[91]

Do the *Solutions* include any passages that resemble this extraordinary feature of the *Homilies on the Gospels*? Question 23 concerns the procession of the Son from God the Father (John 8:42) and the procession of the Holy Spirit (John 15:26) and asks what the difference is between the two. In Solution 23, Hildegard first responds using direct speech with no prefatory identification of the speaker and then comments on those words in the third person. Upon close reading, the unidentified speaker's identity becomes clear. The speaker says, "My Father is power, and *I*, sounding forth his Word, *proceeded* from him when he created all creatures through me. *The* Holy *Spirit proceeded* from him, namely, my Father, when I came down into the womb of the Virgin, whose flesh was not wounded by the serpent's deception. I donned humanity from her after I had been conceived by the same Holy Spirit."[92]

Clearly Hildegard speaks in the voice of Christ, who explains his procession from the Father and his role at the creation, echoing Hildegard's profound belief, characteristic of much of twelfth-century Christology, that Father and Son were one even at the beginning of time. In the voice of the Son, she also explains the incarnation and the Holy Spirit's role in Christ's conception. After that point, Hildegard moves away

---

[91] Kienzle, *Hildegard's Gospel Homilies*, 132–35. Examples include *Homilies on the Gospels*, 1.30–33, on Luke 16:1-19, in which Hildegard speaks in the voices of God, Adam, and Jesus; 11.65–66, on Matt 2:13-18, in which Hildegard takes God's voice; and 26.118–22, on Luke 15:11-32, in which Hildegard speaks as the older brother in the parable of the prodigal son.

[92] *Solutions* 23, 69–70, *Solutiones* 23, PL 197:1047CD: *Pater meus, potestas est. Et ego sonans Verbum suum, ab eo processi, quando omnes creaturas per me creavit: et Spiritus sanctus ab ipso, scilicet Patre meo, processit; quoniam ego in uterum Virginis, cujus caro serpentina deceptione vulnerata non est, descendebam, et humanitatem ex ipsa, de eodem Spiritu sancto conceptam, indui.*

from Christ's voice and, in the third person, begins to explain the mystery of the Trinity. It is as if she were explicating the words of Christ with her own. She is, however, supplying both Christ's words and the explanation of those words. Hildegard explains that the fiery Spirit, which aided in the creation of all matter by the Son of God, proceeded from the Father. She further explains that the Spirit, with the same fire, impregnated the Virgin Mary, so that the Son was born without being begotten by a carnal father. She goes on to explain the human body and human soul, which cannot be seen with carnal eyes, by means of the two natures of Christ, whose humanity was seen and whose divinity is invisible.

This solution and its forceful theological message, bolstered by Hildegard's speech in Jesus' voice, takes us back to the topic of Hildegard and the schools. Hildegard championed monastic learning and spirituality over the approaches of the masters, and her secretary Volmar remarked in 1170 that modern scholastics misused the knowledge given them from above.[93] While this complaint is a general theme of twelfth-century and other monastic literature, the implicit principal target of Hildegard and her secretary's hostility may still have been Peter Abelard. Recall that Hildegard dates her first exegetical vision to 1141, a year after Bernard confronted Abelard at Sens and launched a letter campaign for the condemnation of the errors Bernard perceived in Abelard's works, undoubtedly in the unfinished commentary on Genesis but especially in the provocative *Sic et non* (*For and Against*), where Abelard presented arguments for and against what Bernard and, in his view, the patristic tradition treasured as the most sacred teachings of the church.[94] Bernard decried Abelard's reaching beyond the limits of human

---

[93] *Epistolarium* 2, 195, 443–45; "A Letter of Volmar," in Silvas, *Jutta and Hildegard*, 87.

[94] Peter Abelard, *Hexaëmeron*, ed. Mary F. Romig with the assistance of David Luscombe, CCCM 15 (Turnhout: Brepols, 2004); *Peter Abailard: Sic et Non; A*

knowing, a theme dear to Hildegard as well. He furthermore lamented what he saw as Abelard's misuse of the writings of the church fathers: "The faith of the simple is being held up to scorn, the secrets of God are being reft open, the most sacred matters are being recklessly discussed, and the Fathers are being derided because they held that such matters are better allowed to rest than be solved."[95] These are common themes of monastic literature, but the urgency with which Bernard conveys his message resounds with a forceful rhythm that Hildegard may well echo in *Scivias* when God justifies her mission by proclaiming,

> The catholic faith now totters among the people and the Gospel limps in their midst; the most steadfast volumes that the most learned doctors expounded with utmost diligence are melting away out of shameful disgust, and the life-giving food of divine Scripture has grown tepid. Therefore, I speak, through a person not versed in the Scriptures and not instructed by earthly teachers; but I who am speak new secrets through this person, and many deep meanings that up to this point have lain hidden in volumes.[96]

Repeatedly in letters against Abelard, Bernard denounces Abelard's teaching in three principal areas and compares him to Arius for finding "degrees and grades in the Trinity," to Pelagius for preferring "free will to grace," and to Nestorius for

---

Critical Edition, ed. Blanche Boyer and Richard McKeon (Chicago: University of Chicago Press, 1977).

[95] *The Letters of St. Bernard of Clairvaux* (letter numbers from the James translation). On the theme of overstepping bounds, see *Letters* 240, 321; 241, 321, *inter alia*. For the defense of the fathers, see *Letters* 238, 316; 239, 318; 244, 325; 248, 327; and 249, 329. For the corresponding letters in *Sancti Bernardi Opera*, ed. Jean Leclercq and Henri Rochais, 8 vols. (Rome: Editiones Cistercienses, 1957–77), see vol. 8 (1977): 192, 43–44; 193, 44–45, *inter alia*. For the defense of the fathers, see vol. 8:188, 10–12; 189, 12–16; 332, 271–72; 336, 275–76; and 338, 277–78.

[96] *Scivias* 3.1.1, 586, lines 379–91 (my translation); see also Kienzle, *Hildegard's Gospel Homilies*, 1.

dividing Christ "by excluding the human nature he assumed."
Bernard summarizes and elaborates those objections to Abelard
time and time again.[97] In that threesome of theological contro-
versies, we recognize topics that Guibert implored Hildegard
to discuss in the *Solutions*, specifically the procession of the Son
and the Holy Spirit from the Father (Solution 24), the relationship of free will and grace (Solution 25), and the dual nature
of Christ (Solutions 1, 6, 20, 22, and 23). We can speculate that
her exegetical authority had now reached such a height that
Guibert and the monks of Gembloux and Villers, the latter a
Cistercian monastery, had asked her to speak to the same issues that Bernard of Clairvaux had addressed so passionately.

The Importance of the *Solutions*

The *Solutions* reveals similarities in thought, language, and
style to several of Hildegard's other works. We have noted
parallels with the *Homilies on the Gospels*, the visionary treatises, certain letters, and the *Causes and Cures*. Further examples
are signaled in the notes with the translation. While parallels
from the *Solutions* to the *magistra*'s other works prove crucial
for understanding the unity of Hildegard's thought, they do
not simply echo what she wrote elsewhere. She does not repeat verbatim her own works or the patristic sources she cites.
Analysis of the exegesis of two gospel pericopes demonstrates
that the Homilies have some connection to the content of the
Solutions but no duplication.

---

[97] *The Letters of St. Bernard of Clairvaux*: Letters 242, 323; 243, 324; 244, 325; 248,
327; and 249, 329. Bernard's best-known and lengthiest arguments against Abelard are found in *Sancti Bernardi Opera* 8 (1977), *Epistolae* 187, 9–10; 188, 10–12;
189, 12–16; 190, 17–40. The well-known list of Abelard's errors, based on the
chapter titles of his *Sic et non*, is found at the end of *Epistola* 190, 39–40. *Epistola*
190, which was published as a treatise in earlier editions of Bernard's works, is
discussed in the introduction to *Sancti Bernardi Opera*, vol. 8, xi–xv. There are 117
manuscript witnesses to the letter and about thirty versions of the list of errors.

In addition, when Hildegard interprets the four dimensions—length, breadth, height, and depth (Question 15 on Eph 3:18)—her reading goes beyond what she offers in the *Book of Divine Works*.[98] Moreover, Hildegard interprets Pauline passages in the *Solutions* that she does not tackle elsewhere that I have found, notably 1 Corinthians 13:1 (Question 14), Paul's reference in 2 Corinthians 11:25 to being in the depth of the sea (Question 17), his claim in 1 Corinthians 15:9 to be the least of the apostles (Question 18), 1 Corinthians 6:18 on the sin of fornication (Question 19), 2 Corinthians 12:2-4 on the third heaven and the nature of prophecy (Question 24), and 2 Corinthians 4:18 on the perception of corporeal and spiritual eyes (Question 32).

The *Solutions* proves crucial to understanding Hildegard's theology. Moreover, it reminds us that her *oeuvre* is remarkably unified, so that the careful study of one work may chart a path for comprehending the whole of her thought. The light that one part sheds on the whole grows in intensity for the works written during her last decade. Central to Hildegard's authorial and authoritative *opera* is exegesis; her work of scriptural interpretation grounds its authority on visionary understanding inspired by the prophets, evangelists, and apostles and takes form in a variety of literary genres and a dazzling range of imagery.

In the *Solutions* and the *Homilies*, Hildegard the *magistra* weaves together literary modes that spring from the structure and images of the scriptural texts; together they constitute both a harmonious voice, *vox symphonialis*, to borrow Hildegard's own term for the sweetness of the human spirit, and a consonant view or *symphonia* of Christian history intended to

---

[98] *Diu. operum* 2.1.43, 329, lines 51–53; 3.2.13, 372, lines 23–25; and 3.4.4, 390, lines 20–24. Two of these interpretations focus on the human body, and the third makes an analogy to the power of God. The reading in the *Solutions* focuses on the divine essence.

praise God and anticipate the sight of heaven.[99] Hildegard's exegetical method draws deeply from her roots in patristic and monastic spirituality and literature. Her range of techniques and of modes for interpretation complements her vision of the human condition: elements of narrative and drama mesh with the thematic focus on salvation history, itself a drama and narrative of humankind from its origins.[100]

The careful study of the *Solutions* widens our perspective on Hildegard's range of exegetical knowledge and methods. The *Solutions* must be considered alongside the *Homilies* and other writings from the Hildegardian corpus that shed light on the *magistra*'s exegetical work, namely, portions of the visionary treatises and certain letters where Hildegard responds to requests for her exegetical expertise.[101] It is indeed

---

[99] *Solutions* 27, 76; *Solutiones* 27, PL 197:1049C: *De torrente itinere superioris aetheris, per quem firmamentum evolvitur, sonus elementorum jucundus et gloriosus existit, ut etiam symphonialis vox spiritus hominis, dulcis est in vita sua.* See also *Epistolarium* 1, 23, 61–66, at 65, line 141; *Letters* 1, 23, 76–80, at 79, where Hildegard describes the soul as *symphonialis*. In *Homilies on the Gospels* 26, 121, Hildegard glosses *symphonia* as "the joy of the heavenly vision"; *Expo. Euang.* 26, 263, line 75: *gaudium supernae uisionis.* In *Homilies on the Gospels*, 27, 125, she glosses *symphonia* as "the report of good praise"; in *Expo. Euang.* 27, 268, line 70: *rumorem bonae laudis.* Peter Dronke compares Hildegard's use of metaphor in the *Symphonia* and the *Homilies*, observing that all the metaphors in a given homily are interdependent, in "Platonic-Christian Allegories in the Homilies of Hildegard of Bingen," in *From Athens to Chartres: Neoplatonism and Medieval Thought; Studies in Honour of Edouard Jeauneau,* ed. Haijo Jan Westra (Leiden, New York, and Cologne: E. J. Brill, 1992), 383.

[100] Hildegard's moral exegesis constitutes a modification to Henri de Lubac's assertion that Bernard of Clairvaux introduced a taste for the moral sense that characterized the Cistercian approach to Scripture (as opposed to the Benedictine) (Henri de Lubac, "Mystical Tropology," in *Medieval Exegesis* 2, trans. E. M. Macierowski [Grand Rapids, MI: William B. Eerdmans; Edinburgh: T. and T. Clark, 2000], 143–53). See the discussion by Chrysogonus Waddell of the Cistercian concern for "interiorization" of the text: "The Liturgical Dimension of Twelfth-Century Cistercian Preaching," in *Medieval Monastic Preaching,* ed. Carolyn A. Muessig (Leiden: E. J. Brill, 1998), 347.

[101] Kienzle, *Hildegard's Gospel Homilies,* 45–46.

extraordinary that the monks of Gembloux and Villers invited a female "person not versed in the Scriptures and not instructed by earthly teachers" to resolve scriptural questions that placed the authority of her *Solutions* among the ranks of the Doctors of the Church, where she now officially belongs. Was Guibert thinking of Hildegard as the female successor to Bernard, a feminine voice that in brilliant and distinctive tones resounded with the central themes of monastic theology and exegesis?

Manuscripts and Editions of the *Solutiones*

The text of the *Solutions to Thirty-Eight Questions* (*Triginta Octo Quaestionum Solutiones*) is preserved in Wiesbaden, MS Hessische Landesbibliothek 2 (the so-called Riesenkodex, cited below as R), written at Rupertsberg.[102] The *Solutiones* is also included in the thirteenth-century epistolary collection of Guibert[103] and in four manuscripts that were copied from the Riesenkodex.[104] Further details on the manuscripts and the ordering are found in Christopher Evans' forthcoming edition of the *Solutiones* and in Albert Derolez's comments on the letter.[105]

The ordering of the questions differs in the Riesenkodex and the thirteenth-century epistolary of Guibert. An appendix to this volume lists and translates the questions as they appear in Guibert's epistolary in order to aid the reader with com-

---

[102] The *Solutiones* are contained within the *Epistolae*, fols. 328ra–434ra at 381rb–386ra, Wiesbaden, Hessische Landesbibliothek 2; PL 197:1037–54.

[103] Brussels, Bibliothèque royale, cod. 5527–5534, fols. 153v–155r; Guibert, *Epistolae* 19, 236–42.

[104] *Triginta octo questionum solutiones*, London, British Library, Cod. Add. 15102, fols. 70v–76r; *Liber questionum*, London, British Library, Harley 1725, fols. 159r–172r; *Triginta octo questionum solutiones*, Würzburg, Universitätsbibliothek, M.p.th.q.10, fols. 37r–41v; and *Responsiones beate Hildegardis super questiones*, Vienna, Österreichische Nationalbibliothek, 1016, fols. 108vb–115va. I am grateful to Christopher Evans for these references.

[105] Derolez uses the Pitra edition for the table he presents, which differs from R and the PL in ordering and content. See Guibert, *Epistolae* 19, 235.

parison of the two sets of questions. The epistolary contains two questions (8 and 10) that are not found in the Riesenkodex, Riesenkodex Question 34 does not appear in the epistolary, and Question 12 in the epistolary provides a solution that differs from the solution in the Riesenkodex.

The *Solutiones* is found in three printed editions. Two precede J.-P. Migne's Patrologia Latina (1855): the first was published in 1566 by J. Blanckwalt and the second in 1677 by M. de la Bigne in the Maxima Bibliotheca Veterum. The Migne edition reproduces the latter.

The Translation

The translation below is based on the Patrologia Latina edition, but we have checked that text against the Riesenkodex and noted the significant variations. In addition, we have consulted with Christopher Evans and his edition in preparation for Corpus Christianorum, Continuatio Mediaevalis so that the translation may correlate with his forthcoming edition.

Beverly Mayne Kienzle

Question 1

How should that which is read *He who lives into eternity created all things at the same time* be understood when it is told that God distributed his works over six days?*

*Sir 18:1;
Gen 1:31

SOLUTION

Almighty God, who is life without beginning and without end and who has held all things eternally in his knowledge, *created at the same time* the matter of all celestial and terrestrial things, namely, heaven, the lightsome matter, and the earth, which was turbulent matter. But that lightsome matter, from the brightness that is eternity, was glistening as dense light that was shining even above the turbulent matter, in that it was joined to it.[1] Those two matters were created at the same time, and[2] they appeared[3] as one circle. For at the very first *Fiat*, the angels came forth from the aforesaid lightsome matter, along with their habitation.[4] Because God is God and human, God created angels before the face of the Father, and God formed in his own likeness and image the human, whose clothing he was to don. Thus also, at the command of almighty God, when God said *"Let it be made,"* every

---

[1] Hildegard uses different words for the effects of light in this passage: *lucidus, -a, -um (lucida materia); claritas; lux (spissa lux); fulmino, -are;* and *luceo, -ere*.

[2] R (Riesenkodex) fol. 382ʳᵃ reads *et*, but PL 197:1040B reads *ut*.

[3] PL 197:1040B reads *apparuerint*, subjunctive, in accord with the *ut*. I read *apparuerunt*, in accord with a reading of *et*.

[4] See *Cause* 1.19, l. 8.

creature whatsoever appeared from the turbulent matter according to the likeness of its own nature. For the six days are six works because the inception and the completion of each single work are called one day.[5] After creation, there was no delay for the primal matter, but soon, as if in the blink of an eye, *The Spirit* of the Lord *was borne above the waters;*[6] nor was there any delay afterward, for God said immediately, *"Let there be light.*"[7]

*Gen 1:2-3

[5] Hildegard develops the theme of the six days of creation and its relationship to the six ages of humankind in her other works. She, like other theologians of her time and other eras, follows Augustine of Hippo's *City of God* in her discussion of the six ages. See Kienzle, *Hildegard's Gospel Homilies.*

[6] In Gen 1:2, *Vulg.* reads *spiritus Dei*, while R fol. 382ra reads *spiritus Domini.*

[7] On primal matter, see Kienzle, *Hildegard's Gospel Homilies*, 202, n. 11.

Question 2

What is it that has been written *God divided the waters that were under the firmament from those that were above the firmament?** Is it really to be believed that there are material waters above the firmament?

*Gen 1:7

SOLUTION

God indeed *divided the waters which were above the firmament from the waters which were under the firmament*[1] because the lower waters were present for the earthly things that were established, just as the upper waters would be present for the higher things that were established. For in the upper waters there is nothing of the sort that grows or diminishes, just as in the lower waters whatever is living grows and diminishes the same way as a human does. But the upper waters remain in their original state, just as God established them, and they flow in their own circle.[2] They are material but not like the lower waters, for they are much more subtle and wholly invisible to our sight. The firmament is solidified from above by the moisture of the upper waters and the heat of the fire coming forth there, just as the body endures through the soul, so that it is not dissolved. But the lower waters from under the firmament are more dense;

[1] For the question citing Gen 1:7, R fol. 382ra reads *aquas quae super firmamentum erant, ab his quae super firmamento erant,* an obvious error using *super* twice. PL 197:1040D reads *sub firmamento . . . super firmamentum,* changing the order and correcting the cases. For the response, R fol. 382ra reads *super firmamentum . . . sub firmamento.*

[2] See *Cause* 1.24, line 7, on the upper waters.

they are the mirror of the heavenly lights, namely, the sun, the moon, and the stars. Those waters contain infinite living beings of diverse kinds, which are born in them and live. Therefore, the duties of the upper and lower waters are different in all respects.[3]

---

[3] Hildegard discusses the duties (*officia*) of various orders of creation in *Homilies on the Gospels* 1.30–33; 22.101–4. In Homily 22 she particularly expounds the duties of flying creatures and herds.

Question 3

Before the first human being sinned, was he seeing God with corporeal eyes, and are we too going to see God with corporeal eyes, since, according to the apostle, we shall receive[1] spiritual bodies in the resurrection?*

*1 Cor 15:44, 46

SOLUTION

In the resurrection, when the human will receive a *spiritual body* and when that same body will be united inseparably to the soul, the human will gaze forever upon the splendid face of the holy divinity with the angels. For Adam, who had been created wise and perfect by God, was filled with knowledge and wisdom above all people, but he never looked upon God in God's own divinity, as God is.* When[2] Adam saw the brightness coming forth from God's face with his exterior eyes, Adam knew by that brightness that God was the true God. For before the sin, Adam's soul had dominion over his body, and he looked upon the aforesaid brightness with his eyes, which were spiritual at that point because of his innocence, something that afterward he was not able to do. He lost that vision in Paradise immediately after the sin, when his eyes were opened through carnal desire by his transgression of God's command, which he had known beforehand.[3]

*1 John 3:2

---

[1] R fol. 382ʳᵇ reads *receperimus*; PL 197:1041B reads *receverimus*.

[2] R fol. 382ʳᵇ reads *quadam*; PL 197:1041B reads *quando*.

[3] Hildegard discusses Adam's (not Eve's) transgression at several points in the *Homilies on the Gospels*, particularly 1.30–33, 9.55–61 at 60–61, 22.100–104 at 102, 24.109–13 at 110, and 39.158–61, where she speaks in Adam's voice giving commands to creation.

Question 4

What kind of speech did God use, and in what form did God appear to the first human being when God gave him the command* and when God walked about *in Paradise* after the sin?*

*Gen 2:16-17
*Gen 3:8-24

SOLUTION

Almighty God spoke to Adam with angelic words, which Adam himself knew well and understood. For through the wisdom that he had received from God and also[1] through the spirit of prophecy, Adam then kept in his knowledge all the languages that were later discovered by humankind. He knew the natures of all creatures fully. The Lord appeared to him with inestimable brightness, unlike that in which any creature appears, and God appeared to him again after his sin, *walking about in Paradise* in the guise of a fiery flame.

---

[1] R fol. 382rb reads *etiam*; PL 197:1041D omits *etiam*.

Question 5

Why is it that God said, *Behold Adam, he has been made as if one from us, knowing good and evil?**[1]

*Gen 3:22

SOLUTION

It is like this: Adam, through his knowledge of good and evil, has something in common with us, but with the taste of the forbidden tree he deserted the good through the knowledge of good, and he chose evil through the knowledge of evil.[2] And again, Adam, after being estranged from us through the serpent's counsel, scorned the good, which he had known earlier through experience. Through the taste of pleasure, Adam preferred the evil by consenting to that which he had not experienced earlier. And again God said, *Behold . . . lest he take from the tree of life and live forever.** God said this again, for God was moved by great mercy over his own work, namely, the human who had sinned, lest the human, thus changed from glory, would live forever in wretchedness. In this way, God mercifully drew the human toward himself, just as the father drew his own son who wished to depart from him.* For God himself continued to love humankind very much, whom he knew

*Gen 3:22

*Luke 15:11-32

---

[1] The verse reads: "Behold, the man has become like one of us, knowing good and evil; and now, lest he put forth his hand and take also of the tree of life and live forever."

[2] The theme of ethical choice, the human capacity to choose either good or evil, occurs in a number of the *Homilies on the Gospels*, notably 2.33–36; 7.50–52; 26.118–19; 43.170–71; and 52.187–89.

45

beforehand as the clothing for his own Word.[3] God also[4] created every creature to serve him, and God assigned for the human a place, from which the lightsome human fell like a corpse into death.

[3] Hildegard employs clothing metaphors in *Solutions* 1.39, 7.48, 23.69.

[4] R fol. 382[va] reads *unde*; PL 197:1042A reads *nam*.

Question 6

What sort of eyes were opened for the first parents? They both saw before the sin, as it is said, *The woman saw the tree*, and the rest.*

*Gen 3:6

SOLUTION

The first parents had spiritual eyes before the original sin, for then the soul had mastery over the body through innocence. But after the sin, when their eyes were deprived of spiritual vision and they were made mortal through the condition of sin, their carnal eyes were opened. Thus through the knowledge of evil, they were doing sinful works by seeing and knowing according to carnal desires, as the devil tempted them.[1] Consequently, they surrendered to oblivion all the glory that they had before. Moreover, they scarcely recollected any of their doings, just as a person who looks upon something from afar is scarcely able to determine what it is, and likewise just as a shadow passes by when it is seen in a mirror.

[1] Hildegard refers frequently to the devil in the *Solutions*—6.47, 13.56, 17.62, 19.64, 21.66, 25.74, and 31.81—and in the *Homilies on the Gospels*, notably 24.108–13 and 25.114–16.

Question 7

Why is it that the Lord says to Noah and his sons, *I will demand the blood of your souls from the hands of* *all the beasts and from the hand of humankind,** and a little later, *If anyone has poured forth human blood, his[1] blood will be poured forth?**

*Gen 9:5

*Gen 9:6

SOLUTION

At the resurrection after the last day, God *will demand the blood of the souls* of Noah and his sons and of all humankind, which is the habitation of the soul, through the clothing of the human, *from the hand*, that is, from the movable nature *of all beasts*. God does not want the soul to be clothed with any body or blood, except that which[2] the soul itself warmed and which has been its habitation. For God, in his mighty foreknowledge, foreknew that the human—the breath of life, which is the soul—would be fashioned with flesh and blood from the mud of the earth, as God later fashioned him. In his same foreknowledge, he will demand that the human be resurrected. He *will* also *demand the blood of souls from the hand of the human being;* clearly a human being who kills a neighbor and causes that neighbor's soul to depart will always cry out to God the Creator with the grief of a wailing voice in penitence through the mortification of flesh and blood. For by the wounds of death, that one forced the departure of the soul of one whom

---

[1] *Vulg.* reads *illius* in Gen 9:6; R fol. 382ᵛᵃ reads *eius*. PL 197:1042C agrees.

[2] R fol. 382ᵛᵇ reads *quem*; PL 197:1042D reads *quod*.

God had created. *If anyone has poured forth human blood,*[3] considering it as nothing, without exuding[4] toilsome sweat over this judgment of God, that one will be judged by either sword or poverty[5] or the loss of riches. If judgment is not brought[6] against such a one, it will be brought against the children and grandchildren.

[3] R fol. 382vb reads *humanum sanguinem;* PL 197:1043A reads *sanguinem humanum.*

[4] R fol. 382vb reads *emissi;* PL 197:1043A reads *amissi.*

[5] R fol. 382vb reads *per paupertatem;* PL 197:1043A reads *paupertatem.*

[6] R fol. 382vb reads *inducetur;* PL 197:1043A reads *judicetur.*

Question 8

What sort of bodies did the angels have when they appeared to Abraham and ate the flour, *veal*, *butter*, and *milk* that he set before them?*

*Gen 18:2-9

SOLUTION

Three angels, who appeared to Abraham sitting at the entrance of the tabernacle, appeared in human form. Just as[1] angels can in no way be seen as they are by humans, the mutable human cannot see an immutable spirit. This is because of the disobedience of Adam, who was deprived of spiritual eyes in Paradise and transferred his own blindness to the whole of humankind.[2] Every creature (and the human is one) has a shadow of itself, which signifies that it must be made new for unfailing life. Moreover, just as the shadow of the human reveals his own image, so too the angels, who are invisible to humans[3] because of their nature, appear visible to the ones to whom they are sent in human form through the bodies that they assume from the air. The angels conform themselves somewhat to human ways and speak to humans not with angelic speech but with words of the sort that humans are able to understand.[4] They eat as humans do, but their food vanishes like dew;[5] when it falls

[1] R fol. 382vb reads *ut sunt*; PL 197:1043A reads *sicut*.

[2] On spiritual vision, see both the question and solution in *Solutions* 3.43 and 6.47, above.

[3] R fol. 382vb reads *hominibus*; PL 197:1043B omits *hominibus*.

[4] R fols. 382vb–383ra reads *intelligere possunt*; PL 197:1043B reads *possunt intelligere*.

[5] PL 197:1043B reads *qui semper super granum*; R fol. 383ra reads *qui super granum*.

upon grain, it is dissolved immediately by the heat
of the sun.[6] The evil spirits employ a guise of any
nature whatsoever in order to deceive humans.
They consider humans' nature and make ready
the vice through which they attack them. They are
able to overcome them in the same way that the
tempter[7] seduced Eve through the serpent.

[6] Among several references to dew (*ros*) in Hildegard's
works, the following are closest to the above passage. Hildegard, *Cause* 2.61, lines 6–7: *Nam pluvia et ros terram in superficie
sua lavant, et sol eam calefacit*; *Epistolarium*, 2, 120R, 294, line
4: *Valles interdum uirent et florent de rore celi et de calore solis,
ac interdum arescunt et deficient in uicissitudine tempestatum*;
Diu. operum 1.4.98, 237, lines 187–90: *Quapropter et leticiam in
se ostendit, atque per feruorem solis ardens rorem etiam de quadam
frigiditate habet, horribilis que in tempestatibus suis est, quia sol
iam ad inferiora declinauit.*

[7] R fol. 383ra reads *temptator Euam*; PL 197:1043C reads *tenta-
tor etiam*. This is the most significant difference between R and
the PL edition.

Question 9

Why did Abraham and Jacob give a command, the latter to his servant, the former to his son, that they place their hands under their thighs when they were going to swear an oath?*

*Gen 24:1-3, 9; 47:29-30

SOLUTION

At the Lord's command, Abraham left his homeland and his kindred; through the wound of his flesh, which was the *seal of faith*, he went forth to fight against the vices, as did the glorious standard bearer.*[1] For through the grace of the Holy Spirit, he was carrying the banner of holiness in front of the others, and through the outcome[2] of his own works he obtained the privilege of highest holiness. Therefore in the oath *under the thigh* he prefigured the holy humanity of Christ; by the ancient plan of almighty God,[3] namely, that God descends[4] from his seed through his humanity, he destroyed the plan of the ancient serpent and freed humankind.

*Rom 4:11

---

[1] The translation tries to capture Hildegard's use of alliteration: *ad praelium contra vitia pugnatorus processit.* Hildegard may be referring here to Saint Paul. Guerric of Igny describes Paul as *dux ille strenuus militae christianae fidelis signifer qui stigmata crucifixi in corpore suo portabat* (Guerricus Igniacensis, *In ramis psalmarum* 2, SCh 202.180). In English translation, Guerric calls Paul "the resolute leader of the faithful Christian host and the standard bearer who was carrying the stigmata of the crucified one on his body."

[2] R fol. 383ra reads *fidem*; PL 197:1043D reads *finem.*

[3] See *Vite mer.* 1.21.384–85, line 21, on God's ancient plan.

[4] R fol. 383ra reads *descendet*; PL 197:1043D reads *descenderet.*

Question 10

Why did the holy patriarchs so greatly desire to be buried in *the double cave*, which Abraham bought from the sons of the Hittites?* *Gen 23:9

SOLUTION

The Old and the New Law are represented by *the double cave*, which Abraham purchased for himself at a price. Just as the soul lies hidden in the body, so the New Law lies hidden in the Old, and in these two caves is buried death, which entered the world through a woman.[1] But the holy patriarchs desired to be buried in that same *cave* because, being touched with the spirit of prophecy, they perceived the mystery of the New Law in the Old. Likewise in the *rod of Aaron*, which blossomed, was lying hidden the mystery of the Son of God in the redemption of the human.* For the patriarchs per- *Num 17:8
ceived the Creator in the creation, and Christ, who was going to suffer, was signified by the sacrifice of the lambs and the rams.

---

[1] Hildegard frequently speaks about the Old and New Law in *Homilies on the Gospels*, particularly in 14.75–78, 16.82–84, 20.95–97, 41.164–66, 47.178–79, and 49.181–83.

Question 11

*Exod 3:2
*Exod 19:18
*see Acts 2:3

Was it real fire that *appeared* to Moses in the bush and did not burn up the bush,* or that shone forth on *the mountain of Sinai,** or that fell upon the apostles in the form of tongues on the day of Pentecost,* or that appeared over the head of blessed[1] Martin celebrating the sacraments?

SOLUTION

The fire that appeared to Moses from the middle of the bush—flaming but not burning—should be believed[2] to be the Holy Spirit; the sparks leaping up are the gifts of different virtues. Indeed, the varying appearance of this fire by no means came down from the lightning of the higher elements but from the fire that is life.[3] The living fire does not burn up and destroy the things that adhere to it but strengthens them by giving them life.

---

[1] R fol. 383ʳᵇ reads *beati*; PL 197:1044B omits *beati*.

[2] R fol. 383ʳᵇ reads *fuisse credendus est*; PL 197:1044B reads *credendus est*.

[3] R fol. 383ʳᵇ reads *igne*; PL 197:1044B reads *de igne*.

Question 12

Why is it said about the ark in the book of Kings, *There is nothing in the ark other than the tablets of the Covenant*,* but it is read in the Epistle to the Hebrews, *Behind the curtain there is another tent, which is called the Holy of Holies, holding a golden thurible and the Ark of the Covenant covered entirely with gold and in which there is an urn*[1] *holding manna, the rod of Aaron which burgeoned out, and the tablets of the Covenant?**

*1 Kgs 8:9; see 2 Chr 5:10

*Heb 9:2-4; see Exod 25:1-40

SOLUTION

The first text said that *nothing* is contained *in the ark* other than *the tablets of the Covenant*, which were greatly venerated by the people of Israel. It was not known that there was more in it, nor did the text seek to understand more from it. Paul, however, who on account of the deep knowledge of his own spirit, enlightened by divine grace, knew more than the others, taught more fully what further secrets were kept in the ark.

[1] R fol. 383rb reads *urna*; PL 197:1044C reads *urna aurea*.

55

Question 13

*See
1 Sam 28:7-25
and
1 Chr 10:13

Is it really to be believed that *Samuel* rose up[1] when the medium[2] [of Endor]* called upon him?

SOLUTION

On account of his own sins, Saul was upbraided and abandoned by God, and he wanted to know from *the medium* the outcome of the future battle. Thereupon, Saul instructed the medium to call forth[3] Samuel to him from the dead, so that Samuel would tell him what he was asking. But in no way could this be done. It would be impossible for a holy and righteous man to tell an untruth after death, because no soul, faithful or[4] unfaithful, once it is released from the body, is able to tell an untruth. For the souls of Samuel and Saul cannot have an equal dwelling because Samuel was a faithful friend of God, while Saul was a rebellious[5] transgressor of God's commands. Moreover, the devil cannot deceive the human through the soul of any human, but he deceives people through a phantom and the form[6] of some other creature. For Saul lost his kingdom with his life, since he had withdrawn from God. Likewise Adam was stripped from the

[1] R fol. 383rb reads *Samuel surrexisse ad inuocationem phitonisse*; PL 197:1044D reads *Samuel ad inuocationem phytonissae euocatus.*

[2] Latin: *pythonissa.*

[3] R fol. 383rb reads *euocari*; PL 197:1044D reads *auocari.*

[4] R fol. 383rb reads *uel*; PL 197:1044D reads *et.*

[5] R fol. 383rb reads *rebellis*; PL 197:1044D reads *rebelli.*

[6] R fols. 383rb–383va reads *per fantasiam et per formam*; PL 197:1045A reads *per formam.* The English translation preserves the alliteration.

glory of Paradise on account of his transgression
and became a son of death. Therefore Adam was
not able to obtain what he was seeking before the
Lord.[7]

---

[7] See above *Solutions* 3.43, 4.44, 5.45, and 8.50 on Adam, and
below, *Solution* 25.74.

Question 14

*1 Cor 13:1

Why is it that Paul says: *If I should speak with the tongues of men and angels*?* What are the tongues of angels?

SOLUTION

Angels, who are spirits, do not speak with the words of reason except on account of humans, for their tongues are resounding praise.[1] For a human being comes to know all things that make sounds through their sounds, and the cheerfulness of the human heart shows in the sound of the voice, which the human lifts up with the soul's breath.[2]

---

[1] Latin: *linguae eorum sonans laus sunt. Sonans* functions as an adjective here.

[2] References to the heart and lifting up are undoubtedly liturgical echoes of the *Sursum corda* ("Lift up your hearts").

Question 15

What is *the length and breadth and height and depth*[1] that the Ephesians should comprehend[2] *with all the saints?**[3]

*Eph 3:18

SOLUTION

By *length* is understood the divine essence, which is without beginning and end. The divine essence has its beginning from its own work and cannot be comprehended by the upward reaching of any knowledge.[4] By *breadth* the infinite power of God is signified, which began from nothing and is not enlarged by increasing or lessened by diminishing. By *height* the brightness of the holy divinity must be understood; it never began to shine forth, and its brightness will never pass away.[5] By *depth* signifies

---

[1] R fol. 383va reads *profundum*; PL 197:1045B reads *profunditas*.

[2] R fol. 383va reads *que ab Effesiis comprehendant*; PL 197:1045B reads *que Paulus optat Ephesios comprehendere*.

[3] This passage is often interpreted as the four dimensions of the cross. See Kienzle, "Preaching on the Cross: From Liturgy to Crusade Propaganda," *Medieval Sermon Studies* 23 (2009): 11–32.

[4] This statement reflects Hildegard's monastic view that human knowledge cannot understand divine mysteries and her criticism of masters of the schools who attempt to reach too high. See the introduction, 17–20, 32–34.

[5] The antitheses in these two sentences recall Augustine's frequent use of antitheses in his works. Christine Mohrmann's classic studies on the Latin of Augustine and Bernard call to mind Augustine's style and its impact on all of Christian Latin and notably on Bernard of Clairvaux. See Christine Mohrmann, "Saint Augustin Écrivain," in *Études sur le Latin des Chrétiens*, vol. 2 (Rome: Edizioni di Storia e Letteratura, 1961), 247–75, at 258–60; Mohrmann, "Le Style de Saint Bernard," in *Études sur le*

that God, by these three aforesaid forces, which are under his power[6] and which can in no way resist him, fights against the abyss of the north wind. All the saints are comprehended in God's brightness; they have loved him and remained with him in faith and deeds through the good perseverance of their ministry.[7]

Latin des Chrétiens, vol. 2, 347–67, at 357; and Mohrmann, "Saint Augustin Prédicateur," in *Études sur le Latin des Chrétiens*, vol. 1 (Rome: Edizioni di Storia e Letteratura, 1958), 391–402, at 397.

[6] R fol. 383va reads *ualet*; PL 197:1045C reads *ualent*. A correction to the plural *ualent* seems warranted here in order to agree with the Latin, *in his tribus viribus qui in potestate sua sunt.*

[7] Latin *omnes sancti comprehendentur* implies both "understand" and "grasp" or "contain."

Question 16

Why is it that the Apostle says: *In him we are moved, we live,*[1] *and we are?**

SOLUTION

We are moved in him with the elements, which we use in such a way that we seek from them all the things that pertain to our use. *We live* illumined *in him* and vivified by the breath of life, through which we know that he is God and our Creator. Moreover, *we are in him* because we shall never have an end of life in the soul, whatever the soul's merits are. Through the soul we fly like the wind, and *we are moved* with the full power of the senses, along with the elements and in the elements.[2]

---

[1] R fol. 383ᵛᵃ reads *mouemur uiuimus*; PL 197:1045C reads *uiuimus, mouemur*.

[2] *Homilies on the Gospels* 2.33–36, at 35. On the elements, see *Homilies on the Gospels* 12.68–71 at 69, 24.109–13 at 109–10, and 25.114–16 at 114.

Question 17

*2 Cor 11:25

Why is it that Paul says, *Night and*[1] *day I was in the depth of the sea?**[2]

SOLUTION

Paul was considering his own toil when he said these words in sadness. Through them he showed that with God's permission he was amid toils and hardships, as if amid the dangers of storms and sea swells, which never ceased to inundate him. God also wanted Paul to grow weary through the shadows of the devil's deception and to be tempered by the great disturbance of illnesses.[3] Yet Paul, strengthened by God, endured all these things[4] faithfully and patiently.

---

[1] In 2 Cor 11:25, *Vulg.* and PL 197:1045D read *nocte et die*, but R fol. 383[va] reads *nocte ac die*.

[2] PL 197:1045D identifies the citation as 1 Cor 11:25.

[3] R fol. 383[vb] reads *magna inquiete infirmitatum*; PL 197:1046A reads *magna in quiete infirmitatem*. *Inquiete* seems to be the equivalent of *inquietudine*, and the translation reflects that.

[4] R fol. 383[vb] reads *tamen omnia ab ipso*; PL 197:1046A reads *tamen ab ipso*.

Question 18

Why is it that Paul says, *I am the least of the apostles,*
when he worked more than the others?*
*1 Cor 15:9

SOLUTION

Paul calls himself *the least* because he was not with
Christ, who appeared in human form without sin,
as were the rest of the apostles, and also because
through the Son of God he was compelled by a
spiritual vision, when his soul was neither fully
inside his body nor fully *outside his body,** to a faith   *2 Cor 12:2
that he never desired to learn or to know.*   *see
Acts 9:3-8

Question 19

*1 Cor 6:18

Why is it that Paul says,[1] *Every sin whatsoever that a human has committed is outside the body, but one who fornicates sins against his own body?**

SOLUTION

Every sin that a human commits against another human upon the devil's temptation, through the power of the senses and through that person's own transitory knowledge, comes about through the devil's craft. The devil sows discord among people, inciting them to wrath and hatred. Therefore that sin is *outside the body.* But *one sins against his own body* if one is driven by the heat of the very flesh in the veins and marrow with unlawful desire through fornication until such time as that one incites the self and wounds the self to the point of exhaustion.[2]

---

[1] R fol. 383vb reads *idem dicit*; PL 197:1046B reads *dicit*.

[2] Hildegard describes male desire in *Cause* 2.114 and 177, where she states, "When desire rises in a person it is aroused from the fire of the marrow" (*Cum delectatio in homine surgit, ab igne medulle excitatur*).

Question 20

Where should we believe that the Lord was when he was not among his disciples from the day of resurrection until the day of ascension?

SOLUTION

God remained visibly among us through his humanity, filling the entire earth with his miracles through those forty days after his resurrection. In that same humanity, which he assumed when he was conceived by the Holy Spirit from the Virgin Mary, he cleansed all the elements that had become sullied through the first human's transgression. Accompanied by a throng of angels with the victorious banner of his power, he had redeemed from hell the once captive* souls of the saints and those who were to be saved. They remained with him in the air, where he sanctified all things.

*see
Eph 4:8-9

Question 21

*Matt 4:11

Why is it that it is written about the Lord, *And the angels came and ministered to him*?* In what way did they minister, or what sort of ministry did they show to him?

SOLUTION

When the devil knew that he was separated from Christ in such a way that he could touch him by no temptation, the devil abandoned him and fled from him, as a person flees from an enemy from fear of being killed. Afterward *the angels* resounded with praises of the miracles of holy divinity because humanity, whose first parents had been conquered in Paradise, victoriously overcame all the temptations of the devil in the person of Christ. Thus the angels *ministered* with praises[1] to the one whom they knew to be both God and human.

---

[1] R fol. 384ra *in laudibus ministrabant*; PL 197:1047A reads *ministrabant*.

Question 22

New souls are newly[1] created out of nothing by the Creator's providence and are believed to be poured[2] into the wombs of mothers with tiny bodies of little beings.[3] How, then, do they contract the stain of original sin, and by what justice are they punished?

SOLUTION

The *potter's vessel*,* once it has been saturated with poison, pollutes all the things that are placed inside it and endangers them with uncleanness. In a like manner, all the flesh of humanity is stained and polluted through the flesh of the first human, unless it is cleansed by baptism and penitence through the pure flesh of God's Son, which he donned from the Virgin Mary. The soul draws to itself the stain of sin, for which it is punished, from the form that God fashioned in the mother's womb for this purpose. God sent the *breath of life**[4] for

*Ps 2:9;
Jer 19:11;
Rev 2:27

*Gen 2:7,
7:22

[1] Latin: *novae animae* and *noviter*.

[2] R fol. 384ra reads *infundi* with *animari* expunctuated; PL 197:1047A reads *infundi*.

[3] R fol. 384ra reads *corpusculis paruulorum* with *-a* expunctuated; PL 197:1047A reads *corpusculis*. See *Sciuias* 1.4, 61–62, lines 48–77; *Scivias* (Engl.) 1.4, 109. In *Cause* 2.76, lines 15–16, Hildegard discusses how the soul is placed into the body and explains that in the way that waters flow into certain places, so the soul pours through the body (*quemadmodum aque in . . . perfundit*).

[4] In *Cause*, Hildegard employs the image of the breath of life (*spiraculum vitae*), which enlivens the soul. *Cause* 2.76, 71, lines 16–22: *Et cum deus spiraculum uite in eum misit, material eius, que ossa et medulla ac uene sunt, per idem spiraculum confortata sunt; et*

this. The first human was deceived by the serpent's
plan. But through the ancient plan of holy divinity
in God's Son, the stain is washed away by faith and
baptism. If anyone, however, without faith and
without baptism[5] has entered into carnal desires
with full zeal and does not repent for this act,[6] that
one will remain[7] in perdition with the people who
have not been redeemed through Christ.

---

illud in eandem massam ita se distinxit, ut uermis in domum suam
se intorquet et ut uiriditas in arbore est; et etiam ita confortata sunt,
ut argentum in alium modum fit, cum illud faber in ignem proicit;
et sic in corde eius sedit. Tunc etiam in eadem massa de igne anime
caro et sanguis facta sunt.

[5] R fol. 384[ra] reads *sine fide et sine baptismo*; PL 197:1047B reads
cum fide et baptismo.

[6] R fol. 384[ra] reads *de hoc penitentiam*; PL 197:1047B reads *ad*
hoc poenitentiam.

[7] R fol. 384[ra] reads *permanebit*; PL 197:1047C reads *manebit.*

Question 23

Since the Lord says about himself in the gospel, *I have proceeded and come from God*,* and it is said[1] about the Holy Spirit, *the Spirit who proceeds from the Father*,* what is the difference between the procession of the Son and the procession of the Holy Spirit? Is the Lord called Son, which the Holy Spirit ought not to be called and rightly cannot be called? What is the distinction between the generation of the Son and the procession of the Holy Spirit, when both come about from the Father?[2]

*John 8:42

*John 15:26

SOLUTION

"My Father is power, and *I*, sounding forth his Word, *proceeded* from him when he created all creatures through me.* *The* Holy *Spirit proceeded* from him, namely, my Father, when[3] I came down into the womb of the Virgin, whose flesh was not wounded by the serpent's deception. I donned humanity from her after I had been conceived by the same Holy Spirit."[4] The fiery Holy Spirit, who is fiery life and true enkindling and equal life,

*see John 1:3

---

[1] R fol. 384ra reads *dicatur* above the line; PL 197:1047C reads *dicatur*.

[2] R fol. 384rb reads *patre*, which fits the content; PL 197:1047C reads *parte*.

[3] R fol. 384rb reads *quando*; PL 197:1047D reads *quoniam*.

[4] Hildegard initially speaks in Jesus' voice, as she does in her *Homilies on the Gospels*. She seems to move away from direct speech after this point, referring to "the Son of God" in the third person. See Kienzle, *Hildegard's Gospel Homilies*, 44–45; Hildegard, *Homilies on the Gospels* 1.30–33 at 33, 2.33–36 at 36, 30.132–33, 32.135–37, 35.143–46 at 145, 51.185–87, and 58.202–4. See also the introduction above, 31–32.

exists in eternity, and through Spirit all forms, which were fashioned through the Son of God, are moved invisibly. *The* Holy *Spirit proceeded from the Father* into the Virgin, who is a created being. By his own fire, he so enkindled her womb that she would be impregnated through him,[5] and she gave birth to the Word of God, through whom all creatures were made, without a carnal father.* For similarly the form of the human is seen with carnal eyes, but the human soul cannot be seen. Yet the human is one in two natures. So too the Son of God, who was conceived from the Holy Spirit in the womb of the Virgin, became human. He was seen by all flesh in his very humanity but was invisible in his divinity and exists as one God in two natures, namely, humanity and divinity.

*see John 1:3

---

[5] See *Vite mer.* 4.24.460–64, line 186, for similar imagery for the incarnation.

Question 24

Why is it that Paul says that he was carried off into Paradise and up to *the third heaven* and that he does not know *whether* this happened *in the body or out of the body*, or *whether* he left his body when his soul was carried off to those places, or *whether* he remained in the body and brought it to life when he arrived at those places?*

*2 Cor 12:2-4

SOLUTION

Paul began to fly by means of the rational soul into ecstasy, where Christ called his soul, much as a human being who sleeps goes about in many places through dreams. Meanwhile, the rational soul heats blood in that person's flesh, lest the curdled blood dry out because of the cold.[1] Likewise the sun, which remains in the heights, shines and blazes splendidly and mightily from afar. Paul penetrated and perceived the miracles of the firmament as God had established it, and he was carried off up to *the third heaven*, that is, up to its brightness, which radiates from the brightness that is holy divinity, in which the blessed souls have repose. There he received such great fortitude from God that he could never again doubt. Where holy divinity blazes, there too are the angels, who are like the sun's rays. Paul did not, however, come where the other angels appear as the splendor of fire and look upon the immutable divinity

---

[1] See *Cause* 2.83–84.75, and 2.295, 182, on blood, heat, and cold.

without beginning and without end.[2] For he would not have been able to bear that higher fire, as the eagle could.[3] Nonetheless, Paul came into Paradise amid the splendor of the angels, who perform their duties with humans; there he saw with the soul and fully came to know all the hidden secrets and so perceived them with his body that he knew in his knowledge that those secrets were unbearable to a human, who is ash. For that reason, Paul is wiser than all the prophets; their prophecy, which they saw in a shadow, was like the honey of bees, because it is multiplied for many uses.[4] For all the things that Paul saw with his soul he perceived with his body. Consequently, he left in doubt *whether* he saw them *inside or outside the body*. Therefore, all his words were profound and sharp as steel. But God greatly tamed him as soon as his

[2] On the frequent use of this phrase by Hildegard, see Beverly Kienzle and Travis Allen Stevens, "Intertextuality in Hildegard's Works: Ezekiel and the Claim to Prophetic Authority," in *A Companion to Hildegard of Bingen*, ed. Beverly Kienzle, Debra L. Stoudt, and George Ferzoco (Leiden: Brill, 2013), 137–62.

[3] This idea seems to be an echo of John Scotus Eriugena's evocation of John the Evangelist as an eagle, in Iohannes Scotus, *Homélie sur le prologue de Jean*, ed. E. Jeauneau, SCh 151 (Paris: Les Éditions du Cerf, 1969), 1, 201–9, and his comparison of John and Paul, in 4.218–21, in his homily on the prologue to the Gospel of John. See Kienzle, *Hildegard's Gospel Homilies*, 11, 35, and 42 on Hildegard and John the Evangelist, and 91–92, 202, 274, and 277 on Hildegard and Eriugena.

[4] On the concept of the shadow and the prophets, see *Homilies on the Gospels* 55.195, n. 13. The uses of honey appear numerous times in the *Physica*, though scholars debate how much of this work can be attributed to Hildegard. See the helpful index in Priscilla Throop, trans., *Hildegard von Bingen's Physica: The Complete English Translation of Her Classic Work on Health and Healing* (Rochester, VT: Healing Arts Press, 1998).

soul returned and sat again *in his body,* because he had fierce habits. In that way he would not learn by his own power, for it does not pertain to the height of the holy.

Question 25

The grace of God and free will, what do they have in common, [and] what is particular to each?

Free will is in the soul, which exists as life-giving breath from God and which God creates according to the form of his handiwork. Through free will, humans, whether faithful or unfaithful, in whatever they profess or think, perceive themselves to have God. Humans turn toward evil, choosing it through their own knowledge just as Adam did, who knew God's command but turned toward evil through the serpent's advice.* The grace of God and free will have this in common, that humans, by the knowledge of good and evil, are able to choose to do either good or evil. With the devil's aid humans accomplish what they have chosen through the possession of free will and according to the appetite and desire of the flesh. Never having been compelled, they are able to dismiss the desire of the flesh. With the grace of the Holy Spirit assisting, humans accomplish what they chose according to the will of the soul.

*see
Gen 3:1-24

74

Question 26

How should we understand what is said, "Did you establish *all things in weight and measure and number?*"[1]

* Wis 11:21

SOLUTION

God so established all the tabernacles of our bodies[2] in the right *measure* so that none of those tabernacles exceeds in *weight* or breadth those who dwell in them. So also the sun, moon, fire, air, water, and earth were established in the firmament with equal *weight, number, and measure.* Likewise the human, who is wholly a created being, exists in the right *measure*, because all the limbs were thus filled through the soul, since the human, as long as the soul is present, can neither dry up nor diminish. Pride, however, which flies above all that God established and which spurns God, wants neither to know nor to worship God. Pride falls into exile from all God's creatures; it is death and has no right measure because it scatters about all things that God in his providence and wisdom rightly disposed and established.[3]

---

[1] For Wis 11:21, *Vulg.* reads *disposuisti*; R fol. 384vb and PL 197:1049A read *constituisti*.

[2] For the phrase *tabernacles of our bodies*, see *Vite mer.* 2.1.69–70, line 74; *Sciuias* 3.1.18.347, line 646; *Scivias* (Eng.) 3.1.18.321.

[3] The vice of pride appears frequently in the *Homilies on the Gospels*, notably in 5.47, 11.66 (personification), 37.152–53, 47.178, and 57.200–201. See also Kienzle, *Hildegard's Gospel Homilies*, 161–62.

Question 27

What is and of what sort is the harmony of elements about which is said, *When the elements change places with one another, do they all keep their own sounds, just as on an instrument the quality of the sound is unchanged?** Does what the Lord says not pertain to this, *And who will make the concert of heaven sleep?**[1]

*Wis 19:17

*Job 38:37

SOLUTION

The sound of the elements is delightful and glorious from the rushing journey of the higher air, through which the firmament is unfurled. So also the harmonious voice of the human spirit is sweet in her life because each element has *a sound*, according to what was established by God. All resound, joined together as one, like the sound of strings and lyres. But the concert *of heaven* does not pertain to the harmony of the elements, which will be transformed with humanity. So too the sun, which is placed in the firmament, shines in this world and not in the highest heaven.[2]

---

[1] R fol. 384vb reads *facit*; PL 197:1049C reads *faciet*. *Vulg.* variants include both. The Latin reads *concentus, -i*, translated as "concert," whereas below Hildegard uses both *concentus* and *harmonia*, translated as "harmony."

[2] Hildegard mentions the elements often in *Cause*; see especially 1.7.22, lines 6–9; 1.39.41–42, lines 23–25, 1–4. On the elements in the *Homilies of the Gospels*, see *Solution* 16.61 and 33.83. The musical imagery is noteworthy here, as in *Solution* 38.88. See also the introduction, 25–26.

Question 28

How should it be understood, *The fountain came up from the earth, watering the entire surface of the earth?** *Gen 2:6, Vulg.

SOLUTION

At God's command, *the fountain came up* on the earth of delight.[1] It waters the earth with all its fruits without variable alteration, as it was first established by the Creator. The fountain does not have the alternation of summer and winter and of other seasons that occur on our earth and are similar to the unstable ways of humankind. Just as indeed the moon is concealed by the splendor of the sun, thus also in the splendor of the brightness of this immutable earth, the sun, moon, and stars are overclouded. On the moon there is nothing that is mortal, and it takes in nothing mortal. If anything came into it that was mortal, it would be choked to death by forces as by water.[2] The earth is watered by the water that flows from *the fountain*, which *came forth* in Paradise. On the earth, however, the heat of the sun is so great that drops of rain explode, just as a large, strong fire does when drops of water are poured on it. The fountain signifies the stable ascent of holy virtues, which are kindled through the fire of the Holy Spirit.

[1] Latin *in terra uoluptatis*, that is, "the land of delight," or Paradise.

[2] Hildegard refers to the moon many times in her works. I have not located the idea elsewhere that nothing can live on the moon.

Question 29

Since it is believed that *Enoch* and *Elijah* were transferred bodily into the earthly Paradise, can it be that in a place of such great blessedness they should be thought to lack corporeal food and clothing?

SOLUTION

God in his foresight appointed that Enoch and Elijah ought to be in that place, where they required neither food nor drink nor even garments. Thus all who have been taken up among God's wonders do not use the things that are at hand for mortals, as long as they remain among those wonders.*

*see
Gen 5:24;
Sir 44:16;
Heb 11:5;
2 Kgs 2:11;
Sir 48:13

Question 30

Why is it said about Jonathan that when he had eaten from the honey, *his eyes were illumined*?* *1 Sam 14:27

SOLUTION

Jonathan was like rich and fruitful land. It is overturned easily with a plow and always sprouts forth useful plants after plowing. Jonathan was mild in his behavior but not in trials; he affirmed gladly what was true and just without anger and without hatred. If someone has character of this sort, the humors within are sound and very good through the foods that restore the brain, the veins, and the marrow. The humors do not arise through melancholy, anger, and sadness with the changeability of varying behavior, because the gift of God is present to such a one[1] and causes that one to germinate and strengthen in the way that dew does when it falls on something. On the contrary, if anyone is weakened through melancholy, that person is similar to the hard earth, which is barely overturned by a plow. Unless such people restrain themselves through the nature of the soul, they have in their character anger, sadness, and contradiction to all righteousness; what is more, they are not able to have joy in what they want and what they do.[2] But those who have the character first described are kind in all their deeds, their flesh and blood grow from foods, and they are strengthened through

[1] R fol. 385ra reads *illi*; PL 197:1050C reads *illa*.
[2] Hildegard discusses the bad effects of melancholy in *Cause* 2.67–69, 66–67.

them. So too Jonathan was strengthened. His eyes were cloudy at first from bodily weakness, but he received sharp vision when, through the taste of honey that flew through the air above, he had greater strength than any honey.[3]

---

[3] On honey, see *Solutions* 24.72 and 30, 79–80. Hildegard associates honey with grace in *Diu. operum* 3.4.11, 400–401, lines 15–19: *Quem autem deceret liberare hominem, nisi igneum filium Dei, qui de celo ad terras descendit et de ipsis ad celos ascendit, et qui rore diuinitatis sicut guttam mellis supernam gratiam super populum suum stillat, ita ut fideles numquam ab inuicem separari possint?*

Question 31

Since evil thoughts frequently go out from the human heart,* how can it be known which of those thoughts spring from the corruption of our perverseness and which are stirred by the release of evil angels?*

*see Matt 15:18-19

*see Ps 77:49

SOLUTION

Thoughts are human and were fixed in human hearts from the first original sin, so that people are stirred to pleasure through them in flesh and blood and in their veins. But airy thoughts are vain; because of them humans choose to have in their hearts and desire to know things that are impossible because they cannot be done. On all sides they fly worthlessly like air. It is written about these thoughts, *The Lord knows the thoughts of humanity, that they are vain.** What is said? Human beings, who soar through rationality and who know these things, which they come to know by seeing and feeling through experience, always examine the hidden things that pertain to the soul and that they cannot comprehend through the corporeal senses. Evil thoughts, however, which come to humankind through diabolical art and go out through the human heart and mouth, are the food of the devil, since the devil swallows souls through them, just as a person swallows food into the stomach. The devil, by his deception and through unfaithfulness to God, makes these thoughts contradict God's commands, and thus he strips the human from those commands. Nonetheless, many may bravely overcome the devil through God's grace, remaining with God through holy works and pure faith.

*Ps 93:11

Question 32

Is it possible for corporeal things to be seen with spiritual eyes, and on the other hand, are any spiritual matters known through corporeal eyes?*

*see
2 Cor 4:18

SOLUTION

Spiritual eyes are the knowledge of the rational soul; they are by no means able to see corporeal things as they are, just as a blind person does not see with exterior eyes but knows and understands what is seen only through hearing. Moreover, corporeal eyes do not have the possibility to look upon the spiritual perfectly. But just as a human's form is seen in a mirror although not being in the mirror, so the human sees and knows spiritual things through hearing words in faith. No spirit is able to be visible to a human as it is in its nature, because the human is living breath from God. God strengthens the human's tunic, namely, the body, by bringing it to life. God does not cease to work with the human. When anyone departs from God, that person will be either in the light of blessedness or in the darkness of punishments.

Question 33

Is *the fire of hell* corporeal or incorporeal?* If, as
many faithful think, it is corporeal, is it not believed to be from the material of the four elements?

*Matt 5:22

SOLUTION

By no means is it corporeal. The fire of hell does
not come from these elements, fire does not come
from the fire of hell, and the fire of hell is invisible.
Corporeal and spiritual punishments are not equal,
just as the body is unlike the soul and as the soul
is not equal to the body, because the body dries
up and dies from corporeal punishments. Spirits
and souls are tormented in the spiritual *fire of hell*,
but they do not die from those punishments. On
the other hand, the purgative fire is not enkindled
from the fire of hell; in it the souls who will be
saved live and are punished. The purgative fire
arises through the judgment of God in accordance
with the sins of humans, and from it many are
truly bewildered and greatly amazed.

Question 34

Do the holy who are in heaven and the wicked who are in hell understand the things that are done on earth?

SOLUTION

The holy who are in the heavenly homeland know all the things that are done on earth, since the things that are done on earth appear before God either through God's judgment or through the angels' resounding praises. The wicked never ceased from their sins, nor did they correct them through penitence. They mock their followers derisively, and they know evil things; from the wailing they emit over the blessed who do not follow them, the wicked understand the things that are good.

Question 35

Are the parables, which are told in so many ways in the gospels, set forth solely for revealing something by a similitude alone? Is this the case for the man who fell among thieves, or the king who arranged a wedding for his son, or the ten virgins, or other parables?[1] Does the account reflect what happened in truth, or are they set forth only to show something by a similitude alone?

SOLUTION

Christ told his parables to people on account of the spiritual vices that often deceive them and also on account of the virtues with which they battle victoriously against the vices. Consequently, they would know through parables that he judges them for evil and rewards them for good.

[1] The man who fell among thieves corresponds to the parable of the Good Samaritan (Luke 10:30-35); the king who arranged a wedding for his son refers to the parable of the marriage feast (Matt 22:1-14); the ten virgins allude to the parable of the wise and foolish virgins (Matt 25:1-12).

Question 36

Since the souls of *Abraham* and *Lazarus* were in the place of refreshment and the rich man was in hell, what should we believe about *the bosom of Abraham*, *the finger of Lazarus*, and *the tongue* of the rich man?*

*Luke
16:22-24

SOLUTION

The bosom of Abraham signifies the obedience that Abraham showed to God by the sacrifice of his son and by his circumcision.* Obedience preserves and sustains all good things, as *the bosom* contains whatever things have been gathered together. *The finger of Lazarus* is understood as the ministry of obedience, which is the substance of God's commands, because obedience teaches all good things; it indicates them just as the human points out with *a finger* what is desired. *The tongue* designates self-will, which brings forth banquets of carnal desires. Through the appetite of *the tongue*, all foods are discerned as what they are, just as the will of the human is distinguished through self-will.

*see
Gen 22:1-18;
17:23-24

Question 37

What of special merit does it signify that Saint Martin was so often shown in the appearance of fire, as it is found in the books of Gregory, bishop of Tours?[1]

SOLUTION

Almighty God, who is love and strength, effused the soul of blessed Martin with a fiery outpouring of the Holy Spirit. Therefore, Martin appeared often in fire on account of the merits of his humility, piety, and mercy. With those he always looked upon the living God with a penitent heart.[2]

---

[1] Fire is discussed in several *Solutions*. See particularly *Solution* 11.54.

[2] Saint Martin prevented a fire from damaging a village house, according to Sulpicius Severus, *The Life of Martin of Tours* (Willets, CA: Eastern Orthodox Books, n.d.), 17; see other fire-related miracles on 31–33, 34. Here Hildegard refers to Gregory of Tours, who relates Martin's fire-related miracles in his various works, including *Libri de virtutibus Martini*, ed. B. Krusch, SS rerum Merovingiarum, 1.2 (1885), 134–211; *Historiarum libri X*, ed. B. Krusch and W. Levison, SS rerum Merovingiarum 1.1 (1937–51), 1–537; *Liber in gloria confessorum*, ed. B. Krusch, SS rerum Merovingiarum, 1.2 (1885), 294–370; and *Liber in gloria martyrum*, ed. B. Krusch, SS rerum Merovingiarum, 1.2 (1885), 34–111.

Question 38

In what kind of body did blessed Nicholas appear to the sailors awake and sleeping, both to Constantine and to the prefect, when he did not appear in his own body? When Peter and Paul and other saints whose bodies were buried in the earth become visible to the sleeping or the waking, in what or which kind of body do they come?

SOLUTION

If this spiritual vision did not appear to humans, they would not understand what it was. Nor would they believe, because they are body and spirit in two natures. The form of God, namely, the human who has one part mutable and the other immutable, could never see an immutable spirit unless it appeared in mutable form, since the mutable form is not brought to life except through the spirit, just as a horn resounds through sound and not on its own. For God signaled the good intention of these saints, just as people look at the signs of the firmament, and he responded to their good intention with good intention.

Appendix 1

Question 1. How should that which is read *He who lives into eternity created all things at the same time* be understood when it is told that God distributed his works over six days?*[2]   *Sir 18:1; Gen 1:31

Question 2. What is it that has been written *God divided the waters that were under the firmament from those that were above the firmament*?* Is it really to be believed that there are material waters above the firmament?[3]   *Gen 1:7

Question 3. How should it be understood *The fountain came up from the earth, watering the entire surface of the earth*?[4]

Question 4. Before the first human being sinned, was he seeing God with corporeal eyes, and are we too going to see God with corporeal eyes, since, according to the apostle, we shall receive spiritual bodies in the resurrection?*[5]   *see 1 Cor 15:44, 46

Question 5. What kind of speech did God use, and in what form did God appear to the first human being when God gave him the command* and when God walked about *in Paradise* after the sin?*[6]   *see Gen 2:16-17   *see Gen 3:8-24

---

[1] Guibert of Gembloux, *Epistolae* 1, 19, 236–42, at 238–42.
[2] PL 197:1040B.
[3] PL 197:1040D.
[4] Question 28 above; PL 197:1049D.
[5] Question 3 above; PL 197:1041AB.
[6] Question 4 above; PL 197:1040C.

Question 6. What sort of eyes were opened for the first parents? They both saw before the sin, as it is *Gen 3:6 said, *The woman saw the tree*, and the rest.*[7]

Question 7. Why is it that God said, *Behold Adam, he has been made as if one from us, knowing good and *Gen 3:22 evil?*[8]

Question 8. What is this that is written, *Will a sevenfold punishment be given concerning Cain but *Gen 4:24 seventy-sevenfold concerning Lamech?*[9]

Question 9. Since it is believed that *Enoch* and *Elijah* were transferred bodily into the earthly Paradise, can it be that in a place of such great blessedness they should be thought to lack corporeal food *see and clothing?*[10]
Gen 5:24;
Sir 44:16; **Question 10.** On what part of the earth should we
Heb 11:5; believe that Paradise is located?[11]
2 Kgs 2:11;
Sir 48:13

Question 11. Why is it that the Lord says to Noah and his sons, *I will demand the blood of your souls from the hands of all the beasts and from the hand of *Gen 9:5 humankind,* and a little later, *If anyone has poured *Gen 9:6 forth human blood, his blood will be poured forth?*[12]

Question 12. What sort of bodies did the angels have when they appeared to Abraham and ate the *Gen 18:2-9 flour, *veal, butter,* and *milk* that he set before them?*[13]

---

[7] PL 197:1042B.
[8] Question 5 above; PL 197:1041D–1042A.
[9] This question does not appear in R or in the PL edition.
[10] Question 29 above; PL 197:1050B.
[11] This question does not appear in R or in the PL edition.
[12] Question 7 above; PL 197:1042C.
[13] Question 8 above; PL 197:1043A. An answer is given here, however, and it differs from R and from PL 197:1043AB; thus we have translated it here.

Solution. Angels have natural bodies just as humans have their bodies, and they are animals just as humans are but immortal because they are not then [*nondum*] humans. Furthermore, those very bodies change and turn into the form and likeness that they wish when they want to be visible, densifying and solidifying those—the form and likeness—as much as they wish. Nonetheless, they are impalpable in their true selves on account of the subtlety of their nature, and they are wholly unattainable to our sight. Subsisting in a simple spiritual substance, they assume bodies when it is necessary; once that duty has been fulfilled, they are again placed into that matter from which they took the bodies that were to be released.

Question 13. Why did Abraham and Jacob give a command, the latter to his servant, the former to his son, that they place their hands under their thighs when they were going to swear an oath?*[14]

*See Gen 24:1-3, 9; 47:29-30

Question 14. Why did the holy patriarchs so greatly desire to be buried in *the double cave*, which Abraham bought from the sons of the Hittites?*[15]

*Gen 23:9

Question 15. Was it real fire that *appeared* to Moses in the bush and did not burn up the bush,* or that shone forth on *the mountain of Sinai*,* or that fell upon the apostles in the form of tongues on the day of Pentecost,* or that appeared over the head of blessed[16] Martin celebrating the sacraments?[17]

*Exod 3:2
*Exod 19:18

*see Acts 2:3

---

[14] Question 9 above; PL 197:1043C.
[15] Question 10 above; PL 197:1043D.
[16] R fol 383rb reads *beati*; PL 197:1044B omits *beati*.
[17] Question 11 above; PL 197:1044B.

Question 16. Why is it said about the ark in the Book of Kings, *There is nothing in the ark other than the tablets of the Covenant;** but it is read in the Epistle to the Hebrews, *Behind the curtain there is another tent, which is called the Holy of Holies, holding a golden thurible and the Ark of the Covenant covered entirely with gold and in which there is an urn holding manna, the rod of Aaron which burgeoned out, and the tablets of the Covenant?***[18]

*1 Kgs 8:9; see 2 Chr 5:10

*Heb 9:2-4; see Exod 25:1-40

Question 17(A). Is it really to be believed that *Samuel* rose up when the medium* [of Endor] called upon him?[19]

*see 1 Sam 28:7-25 and 1 Chr 10:13

Question 17(B). Why is it said about Jonathan that when he had eaten from the honey, *his eyes were illumined?***[20]

*1 Sam 14:27

Question 18. Why is it that Paul says that he was carried off into Paradise and up to *the third heaven* and that he does not know *whether* this happened *in the body or out of the body*, or whether he left his body and arrived at those places while remaining in the body and bringing it to life?***[21]

*2 Cor 12:2-4

Question 19. Why is it that Paul says, *Every sin whatsoever that a human has committed is outside the body, but one who fornicates sins against his own body?**

*1 Cor 6:18

Question 20. Why is it that Paul says, *If I should speak with the tongues of men and angels?** What are the tongues of angels?[22]

*1 Cor 13:1

---

[18] Question 12 above; PL 197:1044BC.
[19] Question 13 above; PL 197:1044D.
[20] Question 30 above; PL 197:1050C.
[21] Question 24 above; PL 197:1048A.
[22] Question 14 above; PL 197:1045A.

Question 21. What is *the length and breadth and height and depth* that the Ephesians should comprehend *with all the saints?**23*   *Eph 3:18

Question 22. Why is it that it is written about the Lord, *And the angels came and ministered to him?** In what way did they minister or what sort of ministry did they show to him?[24]   *Matt 4:11

Question 23. Where should we believe that the Lord was from the day of resurrection until the day of ascension when he was not among his disciples?[25]

Question 24. New souls are newly created out of nothing by the Creator's providence and are believed to be poured into the wombs of mothers with tiny bodies of little beings. How, then, do they contract the stain of original sin, and by what justice are they punished?[26]

Question 25(A). Why is it that the apostle says, *In him we are moved, we live, and we are?**27*   *Acts 17:28

Question 25(B). Why is it that Paul says, *Night and day I was in the depth of the sea?**28*   *2 Cor 11:25

Question 25(C). Why is it that Paul says, *I am the least of the apostles,* when he worked more than the others?**29*   *1 Cor 15:9

Question 26. Since the Lord says about himself in the gospel, *I have proceeded and come from God,**   *John 8:42

[23] Question 15 above; PL 197:1045B.
[24] Question 21 above; PL 197:1046D.
[25] Question 20 above; PL 197:1040C.
[26] Question 22 above; PL 197:1047A.
[27] Question 16 above; PL 197:1045C.
[28] Question 17 above; PL 197:1045D.
[29] Question 18 above; PL 197:1046A.

and it is said about the Holy Spirit, *the Spirit who proceeds from the Father,** what is the difference between the procession of the Son and the procession of the Holy Spirit? Is the Lord called Son, which the Holy Spirit ought not to be called and rightly cannot be called? What is the distinction between the generation of the Son and the procession of the Holy Spirit when both come about from the Father?[30]

*John 15:26

Question 27. The grace of God and free will, what do they have in common [and] what is particular to each?[31]

Question 28. How should we understand what is said, did you establish *all things in weight and measure and number?*[32]

Question 29(A). What is and of what sort is the harmony of elements about which is said, *When the elements change places with one another, do they all keep their own sounds, just as on an instrument the quality of the sound is unchanged?** Does what the Lord says not pertain to this, *And who will make the concert of heaven sleep?**[33]

*Wis 19:17

*Job 38:37

Question 29(B). Since evil thoughts frequently go out from the human heart,* how can it be known which of those thoughts spring from the corruption of our perverseness and which are stirred by the release of evil angels?*[34]

*see
Matt 15:18-19

*See Ps 77:49

---

[30] Question 23 above; PL 197:1047C.
[31] Question 25 above; PL 197:1048D.
[32] Question 26 above; PL 197:1049A.
[33] Question 27 above; PL 197:1049C.
[34] Question 31 above; PL 197:1051A.

Question 30. Is it possible for corporeal things to be seen with spiritual eyes, and, on the other hand, are any spiritual matters known through corporeal eyes?*[35]

*see
2 Cor 4:18

Question 31. Is *the fire of hell* corporeal or incorporeal?* If, as many faithful think, it is corporeal, is it not believed to be from the material of the four elements?[36]

*Matt 5:22

Question 32. Are the parables, which are told in so many ways in the gospels, set forth solely for revealing something by a similitude alone? Is this the case for the man who fell among thieves, or the king who arranged a wedding for his son, or the ten virgins, or other parables?* Does the account reflect what happened in truth, or are they set forth only to show something by a similitude alone?[37]

*Luke 10:30-35; Matt 22:1-14; Matt 25:1-12

Question 33. Since the souls of *Abraham* and *Lazarus* were in the place of refreshment and the rich man was in hell, what should we believe about *the bosom of Abraham, the finger of Lazarus,* and *the tongue* of the rich man?*[38]

*Luke
16:22-24

Question 34. What of special merit does it signify that Saint Martin was so often shown in the appearance of fire, as is found in the books of Gregory, bishop of Tours?[39]

Question 35. In what kind of body did blessed Nicholas appear to the sailors awake and sleeping, both to Constantine and to the prefect, when he did

[35] Question 32 above; PL 197:1051C.
[36] Question 33 above; PL 197:1051D.
[37] Question 35 above; PL 197:1052B.
[38] Question 36 above; PL 197:1052C.
[39] Question 37 above; PL 197:1052D.

not appear in his own body? In what or which kind of body do Peter and Paul come, and other saints whose bodies were buried in the earth, when they become visible to the sleeping or the waking?[40]

Note that Questions 8 and 10 above are not in R or in the PL edition. Question 34 in R and in the PL edition (197:1052A) is not in G: "Do the holy who are in heaven and the wicked who are in hell understand the things that are done on earth?"

[40] Question 38 above; PL 197:1053D.

Appendix 2

TABLE OF SCRIPTURAL PASSAGES AND TOPICS

The table below lists the scriptural passages cited for each question. In a few cases, no Scripture is cited and only the topic is indicated. At times, Hildegard introduces other scriptural passages in her solution; those are also indicated for the solution.

Question/Solution Number	Scriptural Passage or Topic
Question 1	Gen 1:31; Sir 18:1
Solution 1	Gen 1:2-3
Question 2	Gen 1:7
Question 3	1 Cor 15:44, 46
Solution 3	1 John 3:2
Question 4	Gen 2:16-17; 3:8-24
Question 5	Gen 3:22
Solution 5	Gen 3:22; Luke 15:11-32
Question 6	Gen 3:6
Question 7	Gen 9:5-6
Question 8	Gen 18:2-9
Question 9	Gen 24:1-3, 9; 47:29-30
Solution 9	Rom 4:11
Question 10	Gen 23:9
Solution 10	Num 17:8
Question 11	Exod 3:2; 19:18; Acts 2:3
Question 12	Exod 25:1-40; 1 Kgs 8:9; 2 Chr 5:10; Heb 9:2-4

chart continued on next page

Question/Solution Number	Scriptural Passage or Topic
Question 13	1 Sam 28:7-25; 1 Chr 10:13
Question 14	1 Cor 13:1
Question 15	Eph 3:18
Question 16	Acts 17:28
Question 17	2 Cor 11:25
Question 18	1 Cor 15:9
Solution 18	Acts 9:3-8; 2 Cor 12:2
Question 19	1 Cor 6:18
Question 20	Where was Jesus between the resurrection and the ascension?
Solution 20	Eph 4:8-9
Question 21	Matt 4:11
Question 22	How do new souls contract original sin?
Solution 22	Gen 2:7; 7:22; Ps 2:9; Jer 19:11; Rev 2:27
Question 23	John 8:42; 15:26
Solution 23	John 1:3
Question 24	2 Cor 12:2-4
Question 25	What do God's grace and free will have in common, and what is particular to each?
Solution 25	Gen 3:1-24
Question 26	Wis 11:21
Question 27	Job 38:37; Wis 19:17
Question 28	Gen 2:6

Question 29	Gen 5:24; 2 Kgs 2:11; Sir 44:16, 48:13; Heb 11:5
Question 30	1 Sam 14:27
Question 31	Ps 77:49; Matt 15:18-19
Solution 31	Ps 93:11
Question 32	2 Cor 4:18
Question 33	Matt 5:22
Question 34	Do the saints in heaven and wicked in hell know what is done on earth?
Question 35	Matt 22:1-14; 25:1-12; Luke 10:30-35
Question 36	Luke 16:22-24
Solution 36	Gen 17:23-24; 22:1-18
Question 37	*The Life of Martin of Tours*
Question 38	*The Life of Nicholas*

Bibliography

Primary Sources

Augustine of Hippo. *De doctrina christiana*. Edited by J. Martin. CCSL 32. Turnhout: Brepols, 1962.

———. *De Genesi ad litteram libri duodecim*. Edited by Joseph Zycha. Vienna: F. Tempsky, 1894.

Bernard of Clairvaux. *The Letters of St. Bernard of Clairvaux*. Translated by Bruno Scott James. New introduction by Beverly Mayne Kienzle. Stroud, UK: Sutton, 1998.

———. *Sancti Bernardi Opera*. Edited by Jean Leclercq and Henri Rochais. 8 vols. Rome: Editiones cistercienses, 1957–77.

Biblia Sacra: iuxta Vulgatam uersionem. Edited by Bonifatius Fischer and Robert Weber. 3rd ed. Stuttgart: Deutsche Bibelgesellschaft, 1983.

Bruno (priest of Saint Peter in Strasbourg). *Acta inquisitionis de virtutibus et miraculis S. Hildegardis*. Edited by Petrus Bruder. *Analecta Bollandiana* 2 (1883).

Elisabeth of Schönau. *The Complete Works*. Translated and introduced by Anne L. Clark. New York: Paulist Press, 2000.

Gottfried of Disibodenberg and Theodoric of Echternach. *The Life of the Saintly Hildegard by Gottfried of Disibodenberg and Theodoric of Echternach*. Translated with notes by Hugh Feiss. Toronto: Peregrina, 1996.

Gregory the Great. *Forty Gospel Homilies*. Translated by David Hurst. CS 123. Kalamazoo, MI: Cistercian Publications, 1990.

———. *Homeliae in euangelia*. Edited by R. Étaix. CCSL 141. Turnhout: Brepols, 1999.

———. *Moralia in Iob*. Edited by Marcus Adriaen. CCSL 143, 143A, and 143B. Turnhout: Brepols, 1979–85.

Gregory of Tours. *Libri de virtutibus Martini*. Edited by B. Krusch. SS rerum Merovingiarum 1.2 (1885): 134–211.

Guerric of Igny. *Sermones*, 2. Introduction, critical text, and notes by John Morson and Hilary Costello. Translation by Placide Deseille. SCh 202. Paris: Éditions du Cerf, 1973.

Guibert of Gembloux. *Epistolae quae in codice B. R. Brux. 5527–5534 inueniuntur*, 1. Edited by A. Derolez, E. Dekkers, and R. Demeulenaere. CCCM 66. Turnhout: Brepols, 1988.

Hildegard of Bingen. *Cause et cure*. Edited by Laurence Moulinier and Rainer Berndt. Rarissima mediaevalia opera latina 1. Berlin: Akademie Verlag, 2003.

———. *Explanatio Symboli Sancti Athanasii*. Edited by Christopher P. Evans. In *Hildegardis Bingensis Opera minora*, 109–33.

———. *Expositiones euangeliorum*. Edited by Beverly M. Kienzle and Carolyn A. Muessig. In *Hildegardis Bingensis Opera minora*, 185–333.

———. *Hildegardis Bingensis Epistolarium. Pars prima*: I–XC. Edited by L. Van Acker. CCCM 91. Turnhout: Brepols, 1991.

———. *Hildegardis Bingensis Epistolarium. Pars secunda*: XCI–CCLR. Edited by L. Van Acker. CCCM 91A. Turnhout: Brepols, 1993.

———. *Hildegardis Bingensis Epistolarium. Pars tertia*: CCLI–CCXC. Edited by Monika Klaes. CCCM 91B. Turnhout: Brepols, 2001.

———. *Hildegardis Bingensis Liber diuinorum operum*. Edited by Albert Derolez and Peter Dronke. CCCM 92. Turnhout: Brepols, 1996.

———. *Hildegardis Bingensis Opera minora*. Edited by Peter Dronke, Christopher P. Evans, Hugh Feiss, Beverly Mayne Kienzle, Carolyn A. Muessig, and Barbara J. Newman. CCCM 226. Turnhout: Brepols, 2007.

———. *Hildegardis Liber Vite Meritorum*. Edited by Angela Carlevaris. CCCM 90. Turnhout: Brepols, 1995.

———. *Hildegardis Sciuias*. Edited by Adelgundis Führkötter and Angela Carlevaris. CCCM 43 and 43A. Turnhout: Brepols, 1978.

———. *Hildegard of Bingen on Natural Philosophy and Medicine*. Translated by Margret Berger. Cambridge, UK: D. S. Brewer, 1999.

———. *Hildegard von Bingen's Physica: The Complete English Translation of Her Classic Work on Health and Healing*. Translated by Priscilla Throop. Rochester, VT: Healing Arts Press, 1998.

———. *Homilies on the Gospels*. Translated by Beverly Mayne Kienzle. CS 241. Collegeville, MN: Cistercian Publications, 2011.

———. *Letters*. Translated by Joseph L. Baird and Radd K. Ehrman. Vol. 1. Oxford and New York: Oxford University Press, 1994.

———. *Letters*. Translated by Joseph L. Baird and Radd K. Ehrman. Vol. 2. Oxford and New York: Oxford University Press, 1998.

———. *Letters*. Translated by Joseph L. Baird and Radd K. Ehrman. Vol. 3. Oxford and New York: Oxford University Press, 2004.

————. *The Life of Saintly Hildegard by Gottfried of Disibodenberg and Theodoric of Echternach*. Translated with notes by Hugh Feiss. Toronto: Peregrina, 1996.

————. *Scivias*. Translated by Columba Hart and Jane Bishop; introduction by Barbara J. Newman; preface by Caroline Walker Bynum. New York and Mahwah, NJ: Paulist Press, 1990.

————. *Solutiones triginta octo quaestionum*. Edited by J.-P. Migne. PL 197:1037–54. Paris: Garnier, 1855.

————. *Symphonia armonie celestium reuelationum*. Edited by Barbara J. Newman. In *Hildegardis Bingensis Opera minora*, 371–477.

————. *Two Hagiographies: Vita Sancti Rupperti Confessoris and Vita Sancti Dysibodi Episcopi*. Introduced and translated by Hugh Feiss; Latin edited by Christopher P. Evans. Paris and Walpole, MA: Peeters, 2010.

————. *Vita Sanctae Hildegardis*. Edited by Monika Klaes. CCCM 126. Turnhout: Brepols, 1993.

Iohannes Scotus Eriugena. *Homélie sur le prologue de Jean*. Edited by E. Jeauneau. SCh 151. Paris: Les Éditions du Cerf, 1969.

Otloh of Saint Emmeram. *Liber de admonitione clericorum et laicorum*. Edited by J.-P. Migne. PL 146:243–62.

————. *Liber visionum*. Edited by Paul Gerhardt Schmidt. *Monumenta Germaniae Historia*, Quellen zur Geistesgeschichte des Mittelalters, 13 (1989): 45–46.

Peter Abelard. *Hexaëmeron*. Edited by Mary F. Romig with the assistance of David Luscombe. CCCM 15. Turnhout: Brepols, 2004.

————. *Letters of Peter Abelard: Beyond the Personal*. Translated by Jan M. Ziolkowski. Washington, DC: The Catholic University of America Press, 2007.

————. *Sic et non*. Edited by Blanche Boyer and Richard McKeon. In *Peter Abailard: Sic et Non. A Critical Edition*. Chicago: University of Chicago Press, 1977.

Peter Comestor. *Scolastica Historia: Liber Genesis*. Edited by Agneta Silwan. CCCM 191. Turnhout: Brepols, 2005.

Silvas, Anna, translator and annotator. *Jutta and Hildegard: The Biographical Sources*. University Park: Pennsylvania State University Press, 1999.

Sulpicius Severus. *The Life of Martin of Tours*. Willets, CA: Eastern Orthodox Books, n.d.

Secondary Literature

Augustine of Hippo. *Augustine and the Bible*. Edited and translated by Pamela Bright. Notre Dame, IN: University of Notre Dame Press, 1999.

Bartlett, Anne Clark. "Commentary, Polemic, and Prophecy in Hildegard of Bingen's *Solutiones Triginta Octo Quaestionum*." *Viator* 23 (1992): 153–65.

Beach, Alison I. "Voices from a Distant Land: Fragments of a Twelfth-Century Nuns' Letter Collection." *Speculum* 77 (2002): 34–55.

Châtillon, Jean. "La Bible dans les écoles du XIIe siècle." In *Le Moyen Age et la Bible*. Edited by Pierre Riché and Guy Lobrichon, 163–97. La Bible de tous les temps 4. Paris: Beauchesne, 1984.

Constable, Giles. *Letters and Letter Collections*. Typologie des sources du moyen âge 17. Turnhout: Brepols, 1976.

de Lubac, Henri. "Mystical Tropology." *Medieval Exegesis*. Vol. 2, 143–53. Translated by E. M. Macierowski. Grand Rapids, MI: William B. Eerdmans; Edinburgh: T. and T. Clark, 2000.

Derolez, Albert. "The Manuscript Transmission of Hildegard of Bingen's Writings: The State of the Problem." In *Hildegard of Bingen: The Context of Her Thought and Art*. Edited by Charles Burnett and Peter Dronke, 17–28. London: Warburg Institute, 1998.

D'Evelyn, Stephen. "Heaven as Performance and Participation in the *Symphonia armonie celestium revelationum* of Hildegard of Bingen." In *Envisaging Heaven in the Middle Ages*. Edited by Ad Putter and Carolyn A. Muessig, 155–65. Routledge Studies in Medieval Religion and Culture. London and New York: Routledge Press, 2006.

Dronke, Peter. "Platonic-Christian Allegories in the Homilies of Hildegard of Bingen." In *From Athens to Chartres: Neoplatonism and Medieval Thought; Studies in Honour of Edouard Jeauneau*. Edited by Haijo Jan Westra, 381–96. Leiden, New York, and Cologne: E. J. Brill, 1992.

———. *Women Writers of the Middle Ages: A Critical Study of Texts from Perpetua (d. 203) to Marguerite Porete (d. 1310)*. Cambridge and New York: University of Cambridge Press, 1984.

Dubois, Jacques. "Comment les moines du Moyen Age chantaient et goûtaient les Saintes Ecritures." In *Le Moyen Age et la Bible*. Edited by Pierre Riché and Guy Lobrichon, 264–70. La Bible de tous les temps 4. Paris: Beauchesne, 1984.

Embach, Michael. *Die Schriften Hildegards von Bingen. Studien zu ihrer Überlieferung und Rezeption im Mittelalter und in der Frühen Neuzeit*. Erudiri Sapientia 4. Berlin: Akademie Verlag, 2003.

Flanagan, Sabina. *Hildegard of Bingen, 1098–1179: A Visionary Life.* 2nd ed. London and New York: Routledge, 1998.

Häring, Nikolaus M. "Commentary and Hermeneutics." In *Renaissance and Renewal in the Twelfth Century.* Edited by Robert L. Benson and Giles Constable with Carol D. Lanham, 173–200. Medieval Academy Reprints for Teaching. Toronto, Buffalo, and London: University of Toronto Press, 1991.

Joyce, Ellen. "Speaking of Spiritual Matters: Visions and the Rhetoric of Reform in the *Liber visionum* of Otloh of St Emmeram." In *Manuscripts and Monastic Culture: Reform and Renewal in Twelfth-Century Germany.* Edited by Alison I. Beach, 69–98. Medieval Church Studies 13. Turnhout: Brepols, 2007.

Kienzle, Beverly Mayne. *Cistercians, Heresy and Crusade (1145–1229): Preaching in the Lord's Vineyard.* Woodbridge, UK: Boydell and Brewer, 2001.

———. "Hildegard of Bingen." In *The Oxford Guide to the Historical Reception of Augustine.* Edited by Karla Pollman and Willemien Otten, 652–55. Oxford: Oxford University Press, 2013.

———. *Hildegard of Bingen and Her Gospel Homilies: Speaking New Mysteries.* Medieval Women: Texts and Contexts 12. Turnhout: Brepols, 2009.

———. "Hildegard of Bingen's Exegesis of Jesus' Miracles and the Twelfth-Century Study of Science." In *Delivering the Word: Preaching and Exegesis in the Western Christian Tradition.* Edited by William John Lyons and Isabella Sandwell, 99–119. London: Equinox Press, 2012.

———. "Preaching on the Cross: From Liturgy to Crusade Propaganda." *Medieval Sermon Studies* 23 (2009): 11–32.

———. "The Works of Hugo Francigena: *Tractatus de conversione Pontii de Laracio et exordii Salvaniensis monasterii vera narratio; epistolae* (Dijon, Bibliothèque Municipale MS 611)." *Sacris erudiri* 34 (1994): 273–311.

Kienzle, Beverly, and Susan Shroff. "Cistercians and Heresy: Doctrinal Consultation in Some Twelfth-Century Correspondence from Southern France." *Cîteaux: Commentarii cistercienses* 41 (1990): 159–66.

Kienzle, Beverly, and Travis Allen Stevens. "Intertextuality in Hildegard's Works: Ezekiel and the Claim to Prophetic Authority." In *A Companion to Hildegard of Bingen.* Edited by Beverly Kienzle, Debra L. Stoudt, and George Ferzoco, 137–62. Leiden: E. J. Brill, 2013.

Lobrichon, Guy. "Une nouveauté: les gloses de la Bible." In *Le Moyen Age et la Bible*. Edited by Pierre Riché and Guy Lobrichon, 95–114. La Bible de tous les temps 4. Paris: Beauchesne, 1984.

McGinn, Bernard. "Hildegard of Bingen as Visionary and Exegete." In *Hildegard von Bingen in ihrem historischen Umfeld: internationaler wissenschaftlicher Kongress zum 900jährigen Jubiläum, 13.–19. September 1998, Bingen am Rhein*. Edited by Alfred Haverkamp, 321–50. Mainz: P. von Zabern, 2000.

———. *The Presence of God: A History of Western Christian Mysticism*. Vol. 1, *The Foundations of Mysticism: Origins to the Fifth Century*. New York: Crossroad, 1997.

———. *The Presence of God: A History of Western Christian Mysticism*. Vol. 2, *The Growth of Mysticism: Gregory the Great through the Twelfth Century*. New York: Crossroad, 1996.

Mews, Constant J. *Abelard and Heloise*. Oxford and New York: Oxford University Press, 2005.

———. *The Lost Love Letters of Heloise and Abelard: Perceptions of Dialogue in Twelfth-Century France*. Translated by Neville Chiavaroli and Constant J. Mews. New York and Basingstoke, UK: Palgrave, 2001.

Mohrmann, Christine. "Le Style de Saint Bernard." In *Études sur le Latin des Chrétiens*, vol. 2, 347–67. Rome: Edizioni di Storia e Letteratura, 1961.

———. "Saint Augustin Écrivain." In *Études sur le Latin des Chrétiens*, vol. 2, 247–75. Rome: Edizioni di Storia e Letteratura, 1961.

———. "Saint Augustin Prédicateur." In *Études sur le Latin des Chrétiens*, vol. 1, 391–402. Rome: Edizioni di Storia e Letteratura, 1958.

Moulinier, Laurence. "Abbesse et agronome: Hildegarde et le savoir botanique de son temps." In *Hildegard of Bingen: The Context of Her Thought and Art*. Edited by Charles Burnett and Peter Dronke, 135–57. London: Warburg Institute, 1998.

Newman, Barbara J. "Hildegard and Her Hagiographers: The Remaking of Female Sainthood." In *Gendered Voices: Medieval Saints and Their Interpreters*. Edited by Catherine Mooney, 16–34. Philadelphia: University of Pennsylvania Press, 1999.

———. *Sister of Wisdom: St. Hildegard of Bingen's Theology of the Feminine, with a New Preface, Bibliography, and Discography*. Berkeley and Los Angeles: University of California Press, 1997.

Schmitt, Wolfgang Felix. "Charisma gegen Recht? Der Konflikt der Hildegard von Bingen mit dem Mainzer Domkapitel 1178/79 in kirchenrechtsgeschichtlicher Perspektive." *Hildegard von Bingen 1098–1998, Binger Geschichtsblätter* 20 (1998): 124–59.

Smalley, Beryl. *The Study of the Bible in the Middle Ages.* Oxford: Oxford University Press, 1952; repr. 1985.

Van Engen, John. "Abbess: 'Mother and Teacher.'" In *Voice of the Living Light: Hildegard of Bingen and Her World.* Edited by Barbara Newman, 30–51. Berkeley: University of California Press, 1998.

———. "Letters and the Public Persona of Hildegard." In *Hildegard von Bingen in ihrem historischen Umfeld: internationaler wissenschaftlicher Kongress zum 900jährigen Jubiläum, 13.–19. September 1998, Bingen am Rhein.* Edited by Alfred Haverkamp, 379–89. Mainz: P. von Zabern, 2000.

Waddell, Chrysogonus. "The Liturgical Dimension of Twelfth-Century Cistercian Preaching." In *Medieval Monastic Preaching.* Edited by Carolyn Muessig, 335–49. Leiden: E. J. Brill, 1998.

Wailes, Stephen L. *Medieval Allegories of Jesus' Parables.* Berkeley, Los Angeles, and London: University of California Press, 1987.

Scripture Index

Topical Index